YOUR DREAM MACHINE

TRUE STORIES OF
CREATING ABUNDANCE

Presented by Jane Willhite

Presented by: Jane Willhite

Producer: Ruby Yeh

Editorial Director: AJ Harper

Print Management: Book Lab

Cover Design: M3 Advertising Design

Book Design & Typesetting: Chinook Design, Inc.

ISBN-13: 978-0-9819708-2-0

Printed in the United States of America

Contents

CONTENTS

CONTENTS

Berny Dohrmann

—— ○ ★ ○ ——

FOREWORD

As I knelt between the candles before the closed casket of the man who had given so much to the field of personal development and transformational thinking, I was bereft—beyond tears. Thomas D. Willhite, founder of PSI World Seminars, had died when his plane crashed at High Valley Ranch, his home and the site of personal transformation for tens of thousands of men and women who participated in PSI's classes. Would his work, his dream, die with him?

Even in her grief, Jane held herself together for her family and the many students and coaches and dignitaries who had aseembled for Tom's funeral. And, for the past thirty years, Jane and her team have held fast to Tom's vision and offered his lessons to more than half a million people around the world.

What do Jane and the other co-authors in this book bring to the world that made her continuing the work of PSI so very, very important? Simply put, PSI training doesn't wear off. The awareness gained and the breakthroughs achieved stay with PSI graduates for a lifetime, because Tom Willhite's teachings go beyond wisdom, beyond personal revelation—they also provide the essential tools and techniques required to make lasting, profound change.

PSI World Seminars is the Superbowl of human performance training—the oldest and the largest tool for transformation.

FOREWORD

Through the PSI mechanism, thousands of people have created wealth, success, recognition, loving relationships and beautiful experiences. So many people, too many to count, have become wealthy; some have even become billionaires. But the true value of PSI is global transformation.

In this book, you will find true stories of the uncorking of human potential. Mediocrity is like the cork that imprisons our potential in the "champagne bottles" of our lives. You'll see the pop that sends the cork to the ceiling as the bubbles of human potential

Simply put, PSI training doesn't wear off.

escape from confinement. It takes something really powerful to jolt an individual out of mediocrity and into greatness and excellence. PSI World Seminars is the number one tool to remove the cork and free the human potential inside anyone, in any country, from any culture across the world, and it has been doing it successfully, for almost four decades.

Jane Willhite has developed PSI World Seminars as a gift to every man, woman and child who seeks clarity of vision, freedom from the prison of mediocrity and the fulfillment of every promise and every dream their hearts desire.

We are so fortunate that Jane and her co-authors have given us these stories, filled with new insights and a vision of unlimited possibility.

Good luck is coming to you today!

Berny Dohrmann
Chairman, CEO Space International
www.CEOSpaceInternational.com

INTRODUCTION

"Strange and wonderful things have happened to me with marvelous regularity for as long as I can remember. People and events of various sorts are forever coming along at exactly the right time to help me move from one interesting world to another."

How would you like to be able to write those lines?

Well, the beautiful truth is you will be able to in a relatively short period of time—if you take the advice you find as you move through this book and make that advice a part of your way of thinking, a part of your way of life.

Earl Nightingale wrote those words in a book that I picked up just a little over fifty years ago. The man who gave me the book told me that if I did what the book suggested, strange and marvelous things would begin happening to me with regularity. And they have. If I were to share with you all the wonderful things that have taken place since I first read those words, it would fill a couple of volumes. I've traveled all over the world, been associated with fascinating individuals and enjoyed good health; I'm a happy human being still going strong, living my dream and doing what I love.

For some reason, I took to heart the advice I found as I worked my way through Earl Nightingale's book, and I began to follow it. Looking back, I think possibly I was tired of living the way I was living. One of the book's greatest truths that sank deep into my mind is that, regardless of what's going on in our life, it can always get better. "Better" is a beautiful word.

Almost immediately, good things began to happen.

The book you are now holding in your hands contains many stories of how individuals have turned their dreams into reality. And although the things they accomplished may be quite different, they all have one thing in common—they are all serious students of personal growth. They also have something else in common— they all have the same potential, just as you do.

Deep reservoirs of talent and ability lie within each one of us, just waiting to be developed. The "dream machine" that you're going to be reading about is your own marvelous mind. The late and great Dr. J. B. Rhine of Duke University was one of the foremost authorities when it came to the mind. He stated, "Our mind is the greatest power in all of creation."

Unfortunately, most people go through life as if it's a practice run. Before you get into the stories in *Your Dream Machine*, take the time to make a list of all the things you would like to have, or the various things you would like to accomplish. Don't spend

*Almost immediately, good
things began to happen.*

five seconds thinking of where the money is going to come from, or how you are going to do whatever it is you write on the list. How you are going to do something is not important. The only important decision you have to make is that you are going to do it.

The Wright brothers did not know how they were going to get their plane in the air; they only knew they would. Edison did not know how he was going to illuminate the world, but he did. Dr. Warner Van Braun didn't know how he was going to put a man on the moon; he just knew he would. You don't know how you're going to get everything you write on your list; the only prerequisite is that you want to be, do or have it. Your age, gender, education and background have absolutely no bearing on your power to turn your dreams into reality.

For the past forty-five years, I have had the very good fortune of working with some of the largest corporations in the world—and tens of thousands of individuals—showing people how to

> *The only important decision you have*
> *to make is that you are going to do it.*

activate their "dream machine" and begin living the way they were designed to live. Everywhere I go, I endorse PSI World Seminars (PSIWorldSeminars.com). It is one of the most complete courses on personal development that you will find anywhere in the world.

I want to congratulate Jane Willhite and her staff for doing such a great job in providing such a valuable service. But most of all, I want to congratulate the authors of this book. Each one of the people sharing their stories with you here is a graduate of PSI Seminars.

And now, as your journey begins, do what I did so many years ago when I made a decision to follow the advice of that book I picked up and allow strange and marvelous things to continually happen for me. They did—and they will for you, if you make the same decision I made.

Bob Proctor
Founder and Chairman
LifeSuccess Group of Companies
www.BobProctor.com

Jane Willhite

THE POWER OF
THE MIND

I n the early 1970s, my late husband Thomas D. Willhite and I
were looking for a property where we could house two-hundred
students and offer our breakthrough educational programs. We
found it in a five-million-dollar college in Artesia, New Mexico
which was listed for sale at half a million.

The college had gone bankrupt in one day, and everything was
left as is. Desks, chairs, typewriters—even paper and pencils—were
all still there. It was as if the place had been created for us all along,
ready and waiting for our students to walk in and start classes!

We decided to move to Artesia, and when Tom went down
to New Mexico to buy the college, I stayed home in Milwaukee,
Wisconsin with our little baby Jenessa. One day I was flipping
through a copy of *Architectural Digest* and, wouldn't you know it,
there was a feature on a house in Artesia!

As I looked at the pictures—the sprawling courtyard, the
spacious bedrooms, the swimming pool—I realized the house
had everything we needed and wanted. "Oh my God, this is my
house!" I said out loud. *I have to show Tom,* I thought, cutting out
the article to share with him when he returned. I kept the picture
on my desk, and every time I looked at it I thought, *I know this is
my house.*

A few days later, Tom called me with news. "I bought a house."

What? He's not supposed to look at houses! We don't even know when we're moving! "No, no, no! Don't buy the house. I want another house," I said, glancing at the *Architectural Digest* article.

"You'll like this house, Jane," he assured me.

"I will *not* like the house. I want *my* house. Let me tell you about it," I replied.

"No, I can't get out of this."

"But I found the perfect house. It even has four bedrooms, and an office!" I said.

"This one has an office, too."

"But the one I want has a beautiful office with an amazing view," I said.

Tom said, "This office has a pretty view, too."

"But the one I found has a gorgeous, big kitchen," I persisted.

"The house I bought has a big kitchen, too."

"Well, I don't care, Tom. You are just going to have to tell them you can't buy that house, because I have found the perfect house, and I want *my house*. It has one thing I am *sure* yours doesn't—a great big indoor pool. I've always wanted an indoor pool." I said, clearly upset.

> *Napoleon Hill's principle "to think*
> *is to create" is absolutely real.*

Tom said, "This house has an indoor pool, too."

"What? Where is the pool?"

"Right off the kitchen," he replied.

"But mine has an indoor pool that leads right off the kitchen! Wait… what is the address of the house you bought?" I asked.

Sure enough, it was the same house. Tom knew nothing about the dream house I had clipped from the magazine, and yet he somehow knew to buy the one and only house I wanted.

The story of the Artesia house is just one of thousands of true stories I could share with you that prove, without a doubt, that Napoleon Hill's principle "to think is to create" is absolutely real.

My stories, stories of friends and colleagues, and the stories of hundreds of thousands of PSI World Seminars graduates prove that this principle, when practiced diligently along with tools that help people harness the tremendous power of the mind, will absolutely help you create the life of your dreams.

I was thirty years old when I first learned the principle "to think is to create." I took a class with Tom, after which we read Napoleon Hill's books. We read just about everything on the market. Up until then, everybody had control over my life but me. I believed my job was to just exist, to put one foot in front of the other and accept whatever came my way. At age twenty or twenty-

People experienced drastic, positive change.

five, I never would have thought I could actually *choose my life;* I wouldn't have gone out there and said, "Get out of the way, I'm going in this direction." No way.

My husband was such a wise man. Tom really understood "to think is to create." Even when we were younger and went to classes with instructors who were some of the best thinkers on transformational work at the time, he knew that where the mind goes, the body follows. It took me a lot longer to really get that, and to shift away from negative thoughts. But once I got it, and began to practice this and other key transformational principles, my mind became my personal "dream machine." With it I could create my life, rather than just let life happen to me.

PSI began when Tom and I developed the class he wanted to teach; three years later we sat around our kitchen table with a few friends and made the commitment to make our dream a reality. And so, the PSI World Seminars Basic Class was born.

The first Basic Class was held in Albuquerque, New Mexico. We went on to Milwaukee, Phoenix, Arizona and other cities, and soon Tom was on the road a lot. Not long after, Tom and I developed advanced classes; in 1975 we moved our operation to High Valley Ranch in northern California.

Tom's class made such a difference in people's lives! Participants started to believe in themselves, if they hadn't before; and if they did believe in themselves going in, they achieved a greater awareness of what they could accomplish. The class brought families together. We had people who came out of the Basic who called people they hadn't spoken to in years—fathers, mothers, brothers, sisters, friends. People experienced drastic, positive change. The class inspired them to be more giving, to consider and commit to their true purpose and seek ways to make a greater contribution to society.

So many people wanted to take the class; it was a real phenomenon. After watching the transformations happen in class after class, I said to Tom, "We have to open this up to the whole world."

So we did.

By 1983, we were teaching internationally and our classes had touched thousands of lives. That year, Tom was killed in a plane crash at the ranch. I really thought PSI World Seminars was over. "He started this whole thing," I protested when friends and graduates encouraged me to go on and keep Tom's legacy alive. I thought about our roles, in business and in our marriage. Tom was the chief visionary, but I was the source of determination.

He would say, "Do you think we could do that?"

To which I would reply, "That's a piece of cake, Tom."

I was one of the first people to really believe in who he was, and who he could be. I held that image for him from the beginning— why couldn't I continue to hold it for him even after death?

So I went on.

Nearly forty years later, we're teaching the same classes Tom put together in 1973. The main context of PSI World Seminars, and its teachings, follows Tom's original message. We have taught more than half a million people the tools they need to truly create the life of their dreams.

Taking the Basic Class is major. "To think is to create" is just the first principle we teach during that class, which is why this is the theme of our first book. As participants go through the class, they begin to see themselves differently, to see life differently. They can see what was once just beyond their reach; things that have been on the periphery of what they want suddenly become vivid. Their dreams and goals are no longer on the outside, hazy and untouchable. Suddenly everything is crystal clear, and attainable: a panoramic view of your life and future, with a clearly marked road that will take you all the way there.

As a young girl I had a recurring vision in which I stood on top of a hill, looking down at a large, beautiful property. In the

> *Suddenly everything is crystal clear, and attainable: a panoramic view of your life and future.*

vision there were horses below, roaming about; I could see them so clearly. I had no idea where this property was, but I knew I would live there. Though I didn't yet understand "to think is to create" and other key transformational principles and tools, I still carried this vision close to my heart.

Twenty-five years later, I stood on top of a hill, looking down at the two-thousand-acre ranch Tom and I had just purchased. This was High Valley Ranch. As I looked out over the stunning, tranquil property with horses down below, I knew that this was the place I had envisioned as a child, the *dream* I had carried with me for years. With the help of my dream machine, my mind, I was able to walk right into the future I had imagined for myself decades before.

I work on manifesting what I want every day. And when I don't get it right away, I ask myself what lesson I need to learn in order to make room for it. From the beginning of my day to the moment I close my eyes to sleep, I am working in my mind to create so many things: new classes, new areas where we're offering those classes, new opportunities for contribution. Everything is "to think is to create." Everything.

Everyone has a dream machine, but many never realize it. Your dream machine is your mind. Whether you are conscious of it or not, with every thought, you are creating your life—why not create the life you desire?

Jane Willhite is co-founder of PSI World Seminars, the leading authority and pioneer in human potential training. PSI teaches individuals and business groups alike the techniques and tools for gaining more control, freedom, power and happiness in their lives, with a focus on communication, self-concept and leadership. Jane is also the co-founder of PSI World, a 501(c)3 nonprofit organization with a mission to do good works and spread the PSI principles to at-risk children and youth. Jane also speaks around the world, sharing her insights into human nature, her personal experience and her vast knowledge of the human potential movement. To connect with Jane, visit www. PSIWorldSeminars.com and www.PSIWorld.org.

Rod Walz

WHY I STOPPED LISTENING

I t was 1979, and my wife Jeri and I were driving home from a workshop when, out of the blue, she asked, "Do you want to handle your money beliefs?"

I'd been successful in many aspects of life. As a teacher in New York City, I'd been appointed Dean of Students at the very young age of twenty-four. When I moved to California and went to school to sell insurance, I was number one in my class, the best presenter; however, I didn't make any money selling insurance. So I moved on to selling calculators. My manager recognized that I had a great skill-set and the right personality for sales, and was puzzled that money still eluded me.

Now I was in the copier business, and again struggling with sales. I was getting by, raising my two children on about twenty-two-thousand dollars a year. Jeri made six times as much as I did, and I felt that difference keenly. I was so frustrated. I had successfully applied the principles of the Law of Attraction in other areas of my life, but abundant money still eluded me. My frustration had come to the boiling point. So when Jeri asked me that question, I enthusiastically said, "Yes!"

We pulled into a parking lot, and Jeri began: "Rod, do you get the principle that you attract to yourself at the level of your consciousness?"

I confirmed, "I believe that."

"So imagine that a woman pulls up next to you in a Mercedes convertible. She's dripping in diamonds—in her ears, on her fingers, around her neck, on her wrists, even on the collar of her fluffy white toy poodle. What's your reaction?"

My immediate response was, "Yuck, it's so materialistic!!"

Jeri said, "You should see the face you just made." She thought that perhaps I reacted to the woman in the example. So she asked me to imagine a man in a Rolls Royce with a big pinkie ring, gold chain and a Rolex watch. "What's the first thing that comes to mind?"

"Probably drug money," I responded without hesitation.

Jeri said, "If that's how you react to people who appear to have money, then how can you ever expect to have money in abundance yourself? You're telling the universe that you find wealth disgusting. And as you attempt to move toward money, it will move away from you at the same speed—because fundamentally, in your soul, *you* don't want what money looks like to you."

The universe is listening, I realized. *I don't want to be like them. Where did this come from?* I started to think about my family's attitude toward money and even how my birth religion, Catholicism, reinforced the belief that rich men had a harder time getting into heaven than poor men. I thought about how, growing up, I did not know anyone who was rich. My family and the people I knew were in the helping professions; they were teachers, nurses, police, and so on. That was the soil in which my beliefs and attitudes about money became entrenched. With this new awareness about where my attitude came from about money, I thought I had hit the mother lode of higher consciousness and realized the truth in what Jeri was sharing. "I get it," I said, thinking I was done.

Jeri said, "We're not done yet."

Jeri took me through a process that changed my life. First she asked me to think about how much money each month would make me happy. My overhead was about two-thousand dollars a month, so I chose three thousand.

She asked me, "Why three thousand?"

I said, "So I can cover all my expenses and take you to a nice restaurant and not feel the bill." She asked me if I wanted three-thousand dollars this month; I gallantly said yes.

Then she asked the killer question: "Are you willing to have that happen?"

I had no idea what willingness had to do with this, so I couldn't answer yes. I was full of excuses, and they spewed from my mouth. "There's a pipeline in copier sales and I've got nothing in mine. I have no leads and it takes time for them to come through."

Over and over, Jeri asked me about what I wanted, and if I was willing to have it happen. Each time, I offered up more limited thinking.

I spent two whole hours bringing up excuse after excuse. Occasionally, Jeri grounded me with the earlier point about attracting results in your life based upon your consciousness, and

*We attract money to ourselves at the
level on which we think and believe.*

would ask her question yet again. Finally, my mind ran out of stuff to throw at her and it shut up. I had nothing external to blame, and nowhere to go but inward. I calmly expressed, "Yes, I'm willing"— nothing more.

Jeri had one final suggestion: "I want you to bless people with money. Say 'good for you,' and bless them." I did.

The next day, the whole world looked different. Grossmont Bank called at 9:07. I'd pitched them six months earlier and hadn't heard a peep since. They said, "Get out here today, because our budget cleared and we're ready to place an order." When I filled out my paperwork, I realized I had just made a twenty-one-hundred dollar commission. Then, later that day, a new customer called out of the blue and I made another five-hundred dollar commission.

Stopped at a red light in El Cajon as I drove home from work, I thought, *Wouldn't it have been great to come home and tell Jeri I made three-thousand dollars in one day!* I heard the negativity in that thought: *Not only did I not do it; I couldn't.* I told my mind, *Shut up—I know you're trying to help me, but I don't need that right now.*

At 4:55 PM, I turned the car toward a building and saw a woman locking an office. I parked and asked her if she needed a copier. She stepped back, a little amazed, and said, "How did you know? Our copier broke down for the third time this week, and my boss wants me to get a new one. Can you come back Monday?"

*Embrace the understanding
that your mind is not you.*

I said, "Yes, however, I have a copier in the car. If you've got a few minutes, I can show you."

She did, and bought that copier right off the cart. When I got back to the car I realized that, with this commission of five-hundred dollars, I had just made thirty-one hundred dollars in *one day.* Instead of reacting with excitement, I realized that I was in the presence of a spiritual process and humbly put my spiritual sword in the ground. I vowed never to listen to my mind again, because I couldn't trust the beliefs that had been poured into me about money.

We attract money to ourselves at the level on which we think and believe. Money is like oxygen. We breathe it all the time—at the level of our consciousness. Notice I didn't say at the level of our ability or skill. All the money that exists in the world flows through each of our consciousnesses. Money is not an object, and it is not something you hold onto. It is a thought that expresses itself as an exchange of value, based upon the value you bring to the world. In the past, we exchanged goats and sheep; now we exchange currency. The real currency is our consciousness about money.

The voice inside your head is not you; it is your subconscious mind, doing its job to keep everything familiar, safe and right based upon the beliefs poured into you as a child, when you had no vote and no veto. Think about it. When did you choose to speak your first language? You didn't. It's as though each of us was given our own unique game to play, in which the game pieces are made up of others' beliefs and our instinctual decisions, as children, to follow those beliefs in order to get love and acceptance. The game is not right or wrong, good or bad; it just is. Unfortunately, most of us think that this game inside us is real. It isn't. You are real, and you are not the game. The game only mirrors your beliefs. Embrace the understanding that your mind is not you. You *have* a mind and it works for you. It will follow your instructions and change its beliefs to be more in alignment with your vision when you take charge.

So how do you control the powerful mechanism that is your mind? For me, it was first by embracing the reality that I had allowed my game to run me. Then I got clear on my vision of what

---

Remember, the game you were
given to play is not real. You are
real, powerful and unique.

I wanted—three-thousand dollars per month in commissions— and declared to my mind, with persistence, that I was willing to have what I said I wanted. I kept spewing out the garbage that was keeping me small until there was nothing left except silence. My willingness was like a prayer to the universe, directly answered by the silencing of my mind.

At this point, some of you might be game but still thinking, "Yeah, but did it stick?" Yes, it did. Roll forward to the year 2001. I'm sitting in my CPA's office, where he and Jeri are discussing our tax return. Jeri writes down my income from the prior year on a piece of paper, pushes it across the table to me with a calculator and says, "Divide that number by 365 days."

My energy calms and tears well up as I realize: *I created three-thousand dollars a day, every day.* I am in sheer gratitude for the knowledge that I have been in alignment with my true power and true self.

A long time ago, you gave your mind permission to run the show. This works most of the time; however, your mind also tends to do everything possible to prevent change. You must take charge of it and have it work for you, not the other way around. Here's a simple technique that I use to take control of my mind by retraining it:

Each time you think of it, tell your mind, "I want you to send me information." Then ask a question—any question, such as, "Recall a time when I was crying." Observe the thought, ever so briefly, and say, "Thank you," no matter what your mind sends you. For example, your mind may have sent you a memory of yourself laughing hysterically. Just say, "Thank you;" don't judge your mind for not sending you a crying memory. Do this again and again and again. After a while, your mind will get used to you giving it commands. You are teaching your mind to recall on demand. You are taking charge.

Once your mind is used to fetching on command, you might do as I do each morning. First, I think of something very specific for which I'm grateful. Then I decide who I choose to be today, and who will I choose to be when I forget, when life throws me a curve. So when the curve appears, and it will, I'm ready to shift my beingness again. Finally, for my relationship with my wife Jeri, I consider what Jeri needs from me today. What level of support does she need?

Spend diligent time on the inner work. Retrain your mind to listen to *you,* and then use its remarkable power to create results in alignment with who you are becoming. Most of all: have fun during your discovery process. Remember, the game you were given to play is not real. You are real, powerful and unique.

ROD WALZ

Rod Walz is a visionary entrepreneur and speaker who has successfully overcome his own inherited, limiting beliefs about love and money. This has resulted in his creation of an incredible thirty-three-year marriage to Jeri, as well as the creation of breakthrough, nationally marketed, industry-creating products.

After introducing the first program used in universities to analyze students' eligibility for financial aid, Rod brought to market the first software system to fully automate foreclosure document preparation in the mortgage industry. He later created the Walz Certified Mailer©, a nationally marketed and patented form product responsible for significant savings in the cost of preparing USPS Certified Mail in over three-hundred-million transactions, and the "Walz Internal Tracking System" (WITS)©, which revolutionized the handling and tracking of inbound accountable items after delivery by common carriers such as FedEx. His company, the Walz Group, focuses on solutions for the mortgage industry and is widely recognized for its excellence in performing services on time with near perfect accuracy.

Today, Rod works in parallel with his wife Jeri's mission to inspire people and organizations to break through inherited, limiting beliefs about money and self. Jeri has written her first book, Where's the Love & Who's Got My Money? The Answer to Having it All. *Connect with Rod at www.JeriWalz.com.*

Kathy Riggs

○ ✪ ○

THE ONLY REAL
PATH TO FREEDOM

*"The primary, fundamental, essential, baseline,
critical, lowest-level minimum requirement for
happiness, without which there is no other hope, is a
willingness to take care of oneself."*
— Brad Blanton in *Radical Honesty*

I remember it as though it happened just yesterday. Walking in
the door, fresh off our trip to the Bahamas, I was in total bliss.
My husband and I had had an amazing, magical time reconnecting
with each other and, though we still had issues to deal with, I felt
certain we could conquer anything together.

Shortly after we came home, I walked into our home office
and noticed a fax on the printer. Immediately, I had this intuition:
When I read this fax it will change my life. The fax was a letter
offering my husband, who at the time was a prominent attorney, a
diversion program for mental illness or drug use. *Drug use? What?*
I looked at my husband and said, "Are you using drugs? Are you a
drug addict?"

"I wanted to tell you, but I was afraid I would lose you," he
confessed. "You're everything to me. I need your help." And then
all the lies started to unfold, and the dream shattered like a house
of cards.

I felt like an idiot. Here I was, a successful executive in a Fortune 100 company, believing I had a passionate relationship with the love of my life. In my mind, I had it all. The truth was, I was married to a drug addict, living a life of lies and dangerous realities. I had no idea he was using drugs; the idea, the image, the reality, did not fit with what I knew of my brilliant, accomplished, charismatic

---

Slowly but surely, he was destroying
our family, one lie at a time.

---

husband. I was in shock. I was angry, hurt, confused and scared, but I loved my husband dearly, and I wanted our marriage and all the promises of the life of our dreams to be true. We had a beautiful daughter and I wanted her to have her father. *How could he be an addict? My own father was an alcoholic and never there for us. This can not be happening!.*

For the next two years, I was completely immersed in the harsh reality of drug addiction and what that means. Meetings and information showed me my own illness of "co-dependency" and "enabling." I learned that it was almost inevitable that this cycle would continue unless I changed.

As part of the diversion program, he was required to go to rehab, and anytime they would let me, I was right there with him. I went to all of the meetings and brought my daughter along to family sessions; I did all the stuff people do to help their addicts get and stay well. Learning what I was learning about myself was not fun. *I got myself here with him, how could this be the truth of me?* I was so angry and scared all of the time! I still was so invested in us finding a way out and needing him to get better first; I would have given anything for him to stop the train and make everything all right. But, no matter what I did, no matter how supportive or threatening I was, no matter how many times I forgave him and no matter how dedicated I was to his recovery, he could not stay clean.

Murderers and drug lords called me from prison with information about my husband, telling me he owed them representation and money, telling me they wanted me to "know the truth" about my husband. Thugs showed up at our house looking for him. He was in and out of rehab three times. All of this kept me in a constant state of drama and heartbreak. Slowly but surely, he was destroying our family, one lie at a time. I felt unimaginable fear for myself and for my daughter. I was helpless and lost, and it seemed there really was no clear way out.

I even broke my own heart and divorced him on a threat around him using again, and of course, despite the heartfelt promises and commitments he used again and again and again. I had to drug test him when he came to take our daughter for a visit. This is not the life we agreed to create. I remember thinking: *I wish I could go to sleep and not wake up.*

Then, I shifted. I met with his sponsor, asked questions, got involved from my heart with the process, and he managed to stay clean for months. He met us on vacation and we conceived our son. I loved him and I wanted to be with him. He moved home

I did not have to look at what I had created, because I could so easily blame him for the entire thing.

(with his sponsor's blessing), got a more normal job and we were pregnant. I adored him, and all I wanted was our family intact. *I just want this to work.*

The thing is, you can't just put a happy-face sticker on a dysfunctional relationship. No matter how you dress them up, the issues are still there. Just because you're happy about it, doesn't make it anything less than what it is.

One day, he offered to watch our daughter, so I could get a break. He said, "Go to church; get some time for yourself. I'll take her to the pool."

I wasn't gone for very long when I got that same intuitive blip I'd experienced when I found the life-changing fax: *You have to go back to the pool.*

When I got to the pool, I found him asleep in one of the lounge chairs and our three-year-old daughter playing around the pool. I sat at the other end and processed my thoughts. *How could he fall asleep at a pool and endanger our precious baby girl? It could be an accident. Maybe he only nodded off and he'll snap out of it in a minute.*

I sat there for forty-five minutes, watching him sleep and our daughter play. *Now I know the truth,* I thought and stood up from my spot. Just then, she ran over to kiss him goodbye and woke him up. When he realized I was there, he said, "I'm sorry. I'm exhausted. I didn't mean to fall asleep."

I realized I could not trust him with her. He could not make good decisions, and now my daughter was in danger.

Not long after the incident at the pool, I attended a funeral for a friend about my age. I was staring at all of the rows of headstones when my ex-husband's sponsor called me. "He relapsed again," his sponsor said. And then he said, "While you're looking at those

---

Little by little, I unraveled the truth of me.

---

graves, I want you to think about one thing: If you continue down this path, he's either going to end up here, or you are. There are only two options for him, and you will kill yourself trying to solve this. So you need to make a choice today, for you and your children."

He loves me, I know he loves me; why must I make that choice? At that point, I was just ravaged. *How much more can I take?* This relationship had brought out a monster in me, grappling for some sort of control and hating the one person that I thought was the love of my life. I knew it was time. The last break was the final break. The night he never came home, I was five-months pregnant with our son and my life was a drama story. I finally understood that no one could save him, but him. And I was the only person who could save me.

Honesty is the only place where anything real gets done. Only in that sacred space can you move and take action, or not, and change anything. Without honesty, you're just chasing your tail—a tail you will never catch. When we practice the principle, "to think is to create," we must first practice radical honesty. Otherwise, we will not get the outcomes we envision.

But it wasn't about my ex-husband practicing radical honesty with me. I had to get real and practice radical honesty with myself. For years, I'd been in victim mode and that was my story. I was the long-suffering wife of a cocaine addict, an addict I adored,

When you're honest about where you're starting from, anything can be created.

an addict who destroyed my heart. This story served me because his addiction was so loud in my life that it drowned out my own issues. I did not have to look at what I had created, because I could so easily blame him for the entire thing. That is just not the truth.

It's so easy to look at the dysfunction of a person, rather than look at the dysfunction that brought you to that person in the first place and the dysfunction that keeps you locked into a codependent relationship. This became evident to me when I attended one of the advanced PSI World Seminar courses. Someone put a quote on the board: "A woman attracts not what she wants, but what she is."

I vehemently disagreed with that statement and told them so! I was so angry. I knew the quote was wrong, because I could prove it. I wasn't the one to blame for my ex-husband's addiction, and I certainly wasn't an addict. So it didn't make sense that I would attract an addict into my life. *You don't know what you're talking about. This is a stupid organization!* That is what is called denial.

The facilitator held her ground, as if saying, "Here, can you stand in the face of accountability?"

At the time, I just couldn't. But eventually, I started to change. It was so hard at first! Realizing that I had been just as addicted to being a victim as he was to the drugs hurt in my gut. Standing in my truth felt as though I was stepping off of a ledge; I had to do it slowly. I would tell myself, *I just have to get through today and a new answer will show up tomorrow.* Little by little, I unraveled the truth of me and then tried to do my best with whatever that was at the time.

All the information in the world is of no value, all the help and advice from others is irrelevant, until it is placed within the context of the power of a person's intention to change. Being a victim is a choice, but a choice we can only see once we have suffered enough. And it is through that terrible suffering that we become willing to do anything, even change and take responsibility for our lives, rather than suffer that pain for one more day.

Only in hindsight can we see that being a victim was a way of looking at life. Granted, a rather insane way of looking at life, but up until now, humankind hasn't known how to live any other way. I believe a huge part of this coming decade on planet Earth will be our learning how to relate to life, each other and ourselves not as victims, and that means taking one-hundred-percent responsibility for what we attract and create.

Many people turn themselves inside out doing crazy, unnatural things to create the image of a storybook family. What I've found on this journey is, that is just a fantasy, a fantasy I bought into and fought to have. But now I know that raising healthy kids and creating an amazing, loving family is about teaching them how to deal with life's hurdles consciously, to love themselves completely so that others can and to live in this moment. It's about the experience you're having with those kids *right now.*

Today, my ex-husband is clean and I've managed to find space for him in our lives as a parent. My children are healthy, happy and thriving. We are a happy and complete family. For so long, I operated under this "life sentence" I felt we had been given and made up a "not enough" story about being a single parent. Once I practiced radical honesty and accepted responsibility for the relationships I created, I was able to choose a different story. We have a phenomenal, complete life. I'm not some dictator who has it all figured out; I simply created a loving home for them. We approach every day fully present and ready to receive the gift it is.

There are no victims in my story now. My children are thriving. Their dad is rebuilding all the damaged relationships in his life and I feel deep compassion for his journey. I know that today I am a different person who is totally honest with herself and would choose very differently.

If you're not honest with yourself, when you can't see the truth that is you, creating the life of your dreams can be quite difficult. But when you're honest about where you're starting from, anything can be created. As Henry David Thoreau wrote, "What a man thinks of himself, that it is which determines, or rather indicates, his fate." Learn to speak to yourself the way you would want your beloved to speak to you. We live in a Universe that is *conscious* and designed to *respond* to the thoughts we send out. Thus, I can be a victim to no one but myself and my thoughts. Bottom line? I choose very differently now, from a place of seeing and owning my true value as an essential part of a very beautiful and ever-expanding pattern of existence! Choose, then choose again, and again, and again and again.

Kathy Riggs is an expert business development strategist. She has been a key part of several multi-million-dollar businesses in the corporate information technology sector and recently launched her own company that provides business planning techniques, education and tools to prepare authentic new business entrepreneurs for ultimate success. Kathy served as Vice President of sales and marketing for TD Mobility, a joint venture company owned by Brightstar and Tech Data. She served as Senior Director, vendor business management, mobility, networking and security, for Ingram Micro North America for ten years. In this role, Kathy was responsible for developing and driving new business models for emerging technology in the wireless, broadband and professional services market, as well as driving the market strategy and vendor relationships in the networking and security category. She holds a bachelor's degree in business science management from Pepperdine University and has worked with high-profile companies, such as Microsoft and Apple. Connect with Kathy at www.Authenticity2Go.com.

Jenessa Meyers

○ ★ ○

TOGETHER

As I rushed around on the grounds of High Valley Ranch, a forced smile plastered on my face, I could feel myself disconnecting. It was the first day of Principia, the biggest event of the year for PSI World Seminars. Soon, we'd have more than five-hundred people on the ranch in Lake County, California, as well as staff, a five-star chef and luminaries, like Deepak Chopra and John Gray.

I was the producer of the event; I didn't have time to be sad. But it seemed beyond my control. I was filled with sorrow caused by my second miscarriage. It happened just two days before the start of the event. No one but our closest family knew; we hadn't told anyone else I was pregnant this time.

The first miscarriage came two years after the birth of our first child, Jenevieve. I was in my second trimester when I started to bleed and an ultrasound revealed that our baby had died.

I couldn't believe it. I remember saying, "But I can see her. What do you mean she's dead?"

What followed was the worst experience I have ever endured. As I birthed the baby who was already lost to us, the pain in my body, head and heart was unbearable.

My husband and I were just recovering from the first miscarriage when we found out we were pregnant again. We were over the moon! But when the second miscarriage happened just weeks after the pregnancy test came back positive, I lost hope. *I may never have more children,* I thought, and that realization was just too much for me.

I was crushed, walking around in a daze with absolutely no time to process the loss, or my fears about the future, or my feelings of inadequacy and responsibility.

My husband said, "Something was wrong with the baby, which is why he or she didn't grow."

But I took the loss as a failure, my mind full of obsessive thoughts about what may have caused the miscarriages. *I'm too old. I've been working too hard. I've been giving, giving, giving, when I should have been resting. I'm too stressed out. I had that glass of wine before we found out.*

My husband wants more children—what if I can't give him any more? I've always pictured having several children. What if that dream is lost to me now?

Growing up, I was very lonesome. My father, Thomas D. Willhite, died in a plane crash when I was ten years old, leaving a hole in my heart that, until recently, despite well-meaning

---

I've always pictured having several children.
What if that dream is lost to me now?

---

family, friends and loving uncles, has never been filled. I was an only child and I dreamed about what it would be like to have a sibling, someone close to me in age. I wanted a confidante, a best friend, someone who, after the sudden loss of my father, could help me cope with my grief and the ever-present fear of losing my mother. I was terrified that I would end up completely alone.

My mother, Jane Willhite, used to say, "The hole in your heart will never be filled until you have children."

She told me that only when I was born was she able to begin to heal her heart after the loss of her mother, and so I believed that my heart would be filled only when I had children. I wanted a lot of children to fill the giant hole in my heart created the day my father died.

When Jenevieve's second birthday was coming up, I became desperate to get pregnant. In my mid-thirties, I knew the window of fertility was closing and so focused all of my energy on getting pregnant. I am a product of my parent's determination and my life reflects the values I have been taught, especially the concept "to think is to create." I knew this to be true, and how powerful it really was—I'd seen it work in my own life, in my mother's life and in the lives of thousands of PSI World Seminars graduates who studied my father's philosophies.

> *"Be careful what you think*
> *because you will create it."*

That old saying, "Be careful what you wish for..." has several different endings—"Be careful what you wish for; you may receive it," and "Be careful what you wish for or you just might get it," and others—all alluding to the possibility of getting your wish.

From my experience, the phrase should be, "Be careful what you *think,* because you *will* create it." It's not about one wish upon a star; it's about your thoughts. And there is no "maybe" or "might" about it.

I know that if I am truly aligned in my thoughts, using all of the visioning tools at my disposal, what I want is not only achievable, but it is also guaranteed. When I want something, I know I can have it—I have a lifetime of manifestation stories to prove it. And it did work. I got pregnant again—twice—but I still had only one child.

That week at Principia after the second miscarriage, I did a lot of internal work. I meditated and read some of my father's manuscripts, but my lack of clarity, drive and connection remained.

Every morning we start the day with a video of my dad talking about the core principles of PSI. One morning, I sat down to watch his video, *First Day, Last Day*, in which he talks about a quote that changed his life: "Today is the first day of the rest of your life. Today is the last day of the rest of your life." He explained that the quote reminded him to live every day with hope for the future, while also living with no regrets, unfinished business or anger. He said the concept would "free you from the fear of tomorrow and the regrets of yesterday."

To hear my father talking to me, sharing just the right insights when I needed them the most, helped me to begin to shift my thinking.

At first, I found it difficult to think about "first day," because I still felt so hopeless. So I focused on "last day." In the video, my father went on to talk about the importance of living a very

There are three steps—vision, implementation and surrender.

clean life, a life in which you don't create drama, or hurt people intentionally or carry around regret. I thought: *If this was my last day on Earth, would I leave any baggage behind?*

Listening to my father's lecture, I realized that engaging my anger, fear and hopelessness was not how I wanted to live my life, even for one day. I thought, *If Jenevieve is our only child, how could I blight her life by wishing for children I'm never going to have?* "Last day" is about gratitude as well, about making sure that the people you love know how much you love them. Nobody knew my father would die that day his plane went down, but he died knowing how much we loved him and knowing that we *knew* how much he loved us.

Wasn't it time for me to focus on all the beautiful people I *did* have in my life, rather than the two I lost?

In the months after that week at Principia, I mourned the people my two babies would have become and started to realign my thinking.

Rather than focus all of my energies on creating a pregnancy, I focused on creating a *child,* a child who would be the perfect daughter or son for my husband and I and the perfect sibling for Jenevieve, the daughter or son and sibling that God/the Universe meant to give us.

I let go of the how. Fertility treatments, adoption—all options had to be green-lighted in my mind. Whether it was this month or in a few years from now, I trusted that it would manifest.

I understood that much more
than biology was at work.

I surrendered to God's/the Universe's plan of manifest destiny, secure in the knowledge that my dream would become a reality. I came to understand the joy of gratitude and being so blessed every day. Two months later, I was pregnant again.

Using the tool "to think is to create" is very tricky, which is why many people get mixed results and discount its effectiveness. It is truly the most highly effective and powerful tool I know, but it's not as simple as just thinking about what you want. There are three steps—vision, implementation and surrender. It's the last step that is so often forgotten or manipulated. When you're caught up in creating your dreams, it can be difficult to remember this last, so important, step.

Despite the more than thirty years of guidance from my mother, other PSI instructors and my late father through his manuscripts and videos, even I had temporarily forgotten the last step. When I remembered, everything changed.

A few months into my pregnancy, my husband and I went for an ultrasound. I sat there with bated breath staring at the image on the screen. I was so afraid we'd see the same lump of black we'd seen on the last two ultrasounds when I miscarried, that we'd hear bad news again. *Just show us the baby is alive,* I prayed.

"Is everything okay?" I asked the doctor.

33

She just smiled and said, "Yes, except… you don't have one healthy baby; you have two."

Twins. We were pregnant with twins! I was in shock, disbelieving. I knew there was a possibility I might have twins— my grandfather was a twin, and my cousin has twins—but after losing two babies, I honestly never thought it would happen to me.

Looking at the screen, I understood that much more than biology was at work. I knew without a doubt that I was looking at the two children we had lost.

It wasn't that I had done anything wrong, or that there was anything wrong with them. My children simply wanted to come together.

In living in gratitude for all life's blessings, in hope for the future and without regrets, surrendering to God/the Universe completely in creation of the family of my dreams, I made space for my children to come to me as *they* intended. Full term. Healthy. Born without complications.

Together.

JENESSA MEYERS

Jenessa Meyers is the beloved daughter of Thomas and Jane Willhite, co-founders of PSI World Seminars, the leading authority and pioneer in human potential training for the past forty years. She has studied the PSI philosophy all of her life. Jenessa devotes much of her time volunteering and sits on the Board of Trustees of PSI World. She is an Instructor for PSI World Seminars, creator of the current Teen Experience and producer of Principia, the pinnacle of participation in PSI courses.

Jenessa earned her degree from the University of Southern California, where she followed her passion as an opera singer. She has been featured in many productions but is currently performing for her daughter, Jenevieve, twin son and daughter, Joseph and Julianna, and her wonderful husband, Jeffrey. They are joyously awaiting the arrival of their second son. To connect with Jenessa please go to www.PSIWorldSeminars.com.

Catherine C. Byrne, PhD

○ ★ ○

MOVING BEYOND "THE OTHER," TO ONENESS

"**D**o *you want to stay, Cath? Or do you want to go? It's your choice.*"

When I was sixteen, my mother and I went to the funeral of some black activists who had been killed in Alexandra, a primarily black township outside of Johannesburg, South Africa. Mostly white churchgoers in solidarity with the struggle, our group took a convoy of vehicles from the Johannesburg Cathedral to Alexandra. (Townships were settled near cities, so businesses would have close access to underpaid labor.) The army and police stopped our convoy as we entered the township by blocking the road with large, scary military vehicles the size of tanks called "Casspirs."

At the blockade, our group leaders warned us that things could get ugly, and families with children might want to turn back. My mom turned to me and asked, "Do you want to stay, Cath? Or do you want to go? It's your choice."

Of course, I was very afraid—I had seen people being tear-gassed and harassed by the police. But I also knew it was right to stay. The leaders of our group negotiated with the police to let us through just to go to the funeral; then we would leave. As we drove in on dirt roads past thousands of corrugated iron shacks, people waved and ran, following the procession as we progressed to the gravesides. The cemetery stretched far out over an open field and sloped up. Above, on a ridge, I saw what looked like a white picket fence. But, as we got closer, I realized it was a long line of police holding rifles.

A police helicopter hovered overhead as thousands of people sang, prayed, remembered and mourned in the dusty wind. The moment the service ended, an announcement came from a police megaphone: "YOU HAVE FIVE MINUTES TO DISPERSE." Just as our group reached our vehicles, we heard the sound of shots. The police were firing tear gas and rubber bullets on the still-dispersing crowd. As we drove out of the township and back to our homes of privilege and quiet that day, I wondered what happened to those who remained.

My parents were very actively involved in challenging our country's racist apartheid system. When I was in first and second grade in a Catholic girls' school—all white, by law, at the time—they urged me to remain seated when we were asked to stand and sing the national anthem, because it did not represent everyone in our country. I didn't understand what it all meant, but I believed strongly that it was the right idea. So, when the nuns came around and asked me to stand, I politely recited my reason for not doing so and remained seated.

On national holidays like Republic Day, festival parades were held out on the sports fields. Orange, white and blue flags flew everywhere, and there were different "fun" activities offered, including a show of how police dogs were trained. Onlookers roared as they watched the celebratory scene: A black person with a large, cast-like covering on his arm ran from one end of the field to the other as a German Shepherd, released by a policeman, chased after him. As the dog pulled him to the ground, the man offered up his cast-clad arm to the dog. The dogs were singularly well-trained to attack black South Africans only.

My parents and I were appalled by the spectacle. There was no acknowledgment of what these dogs were actually being used for in our society, but I knew because my parents told me. They didn't want me to go to these events or to have to walk in parades with the national flag symbolizing apartheid. Friends at school told me their parents wouldn't let them play with me, because we were "Communists." They didn't even know what the word meant. Yes, our family had black friends and went to church in the nearby black township. And yes, we believed what was happening was deeply wrong and tried to do something about it.

We visited activists in prison to offer support and let the police know they couldn't just "disappear" people without it being noticed. Our phones were tapped and, though my father made it

*I realized it was a long line
of police holding rifles.*

into a joke, it was frightening to know we were being watched. Far more frightening, however, was the knowledge that our friends, and other fellow human beings, had no protection from state-sanctioned violence.

It was very clear to me that I experienced many layers of white privilege—I had or would have a good education, food, running water, electricity, the right to vote and access to certain jobs. Our family had money, a housekeeper and a gardener. I could move around the country freely; I didn't have to carry ID. I was not monitored in shops as an assumed shoplifter. I would ask my mom, "Why was I born white? Why was I born privileged? Why are some people born black and others white?"

She would say, "It is an accident of birth." Indeed, my birth as a white person was an accident, but what we do with our privilege should be no accident. My parents taught me to acknowledge my privilege and use it to benefit others less so.

All human beings matter. And our bodies are sacred. They are our own—they belong to each one of us, not to those around us. If only we could all universally remember this one moral guideline, things could be so different in our homes, our communities and the world. No one has the right to invade another person's body. If we remembered this, nobody would be physically or sexually abused. Nobody would be stabbed, shot or beaten. Nobody would be tortured, disappeared or killed by any individual, group, state or nation. We have lost our way. Who are we to think we have the right to do these things to each other? Where did we get this idea?

I believe that we are all, in essence, good; we simply forget our Oneness as human beings. We are all connected in our humanity. We are the same, no matter how different we may look or sound from one another. And world peace is possible. But most of us—if we look within—have become jaded and given up on creating

We believed what was happening was deeply wrong and tried to do something about it.

this possibility. World peace IS possible in our lifetime if we hold a clear vision of it and work intentionally together to make it a reality. We must begin with a vision of humanity that holds, as its moral basis, the treatment of each human being—in each human body—as both sacred and equal.

I have already seen the triumph of such a dedicated vision and struggle in South Africa, where Nelson Mandela, jailed as a political prisoner for almost thirty years, eventually became President. When I was a child, however, it was hard to even conceive of his release from prison, much less his presidency. He had been in prison since long before I was born; and for generations, the white apartheid government oppressed our country's majority population of black South Africans with violent military force, systems of segregation and poverty and denial of their basic human rights, including the right to vote.

If we understand the Oneness of humanity, we can create a more just world where there is ENOUGH for EVERYONE—for we lack not resources, but only the fair distribution of them.

It is so important to remember that mere thoughts initially CREATED this frightening continuum of hate and suffering in my home country. Judgments became prejudice, then acts of discrimination, then acts of violence; all of this led to black South

Africans being regarded as non-human, thus undeserving of human rights.

I was twenty when Mandela was released, twenty-four when he became president. It seemed so fast to me then. But I realize now that fifty years of Mandela's personal struggle occurred before I was even born. The change didn't come quickly or without a lot of work, vision, organization, strategy, sacrifice and family loss by thousands of people with differing views, not to mention international economic pressure. Positive thought and vision indeed create and lead to change, but change also requires great courage and capacity for action.

We can strengthen the change and move it forward, but we dare not forget the suffering and sacrifice by so many generations that brought us to the point of historical manifestation of a more just society—lest we forget and lose our way again and allow thoughts to create new systems of prejudice, discrimination and

> *We are all creating our lives, all the time, with our thoughts. So, we need to be careful what we are thinking.*

violent oppression. Great change on a societal level takes a shift in consciousness of many people, from varied political perspectives, at different rates over time. If we become too critical of how and when and what change should look like, we'll lose sight of the end goal and become despondent. We need to remember that what we're going for is the right idea and maintain that peace is possible in our lifetime.

Only we can make it happen now. We are all creating our lives, all the time, with our thoughts. So, we need to be careful what we are thinking. If we can at least hold each person's body as sacred no matter what his or her beliefs or opinions may be, it might help us to remember that we are ALL human beings, that we all matter, that we are all connected and that there is no need to kill or hurt each other over "different ideologies and beliefs." May we let that thought, that principle, be our guide in creating a world of harmony, equality and justice.

On February 11, 1990, Nelson Mandela was released from prison at the age of seventy-one, after more than twenty-seven years in jail. It was unbelievably exciting. I had just returned to South Africa after a year in the United States as an exchange student, and a ton of friends gathered to celebrate in our garden, many of them black South Africans. Everyone sang and shouted with joy! Many whites in the country were not so excited and were somewhat scared. They didn't know what it would mean. For them, Mandela wasn't a hero; he was a political terrorist. I, however, was thrilled, yet in utter disbelief that it had actually happened!

Neither of my parents lived to see Mandela become President of a new South Africa four years after his release. Because this was the first time black South Africans were allowed to vote, the election took several days as thousands upon thousands of people streamed to the polls in lines that snaked for miles. I read later that an elderly black woman told Mandela, "We feel like human beings for the first time in our lives."

The day Mandela was inaugurated—April 27, 1994—I was back studying in Oregon as an undergraduate. Large screens were set up at the university, and we watched as Mandela stood in front of the government buildings that for generations had represented the stronghold of the apartheid regime. Watching him take ownership of the buildings, the country, the nation, was deeply emotional. When I got to actually shake his hand in Cape Town a year later, I kept my arm out of the bath that night. I couldn't bear to wash off the physical presence of the man who had shown me what persistent vision could truly make possible—he activated those capacities within himself even under the darkest of circumstances, and we can do the same.

CATHERINE C. BYRNE, PHD

Catherine C. Byrne, PhD, holds a doctorate in social psychology, and a master's degree in international peace studies. She held a tenure-track position at the University of California, Santa Cruz (UCSC) in the psychology department from 2004 to 2007, then chose to leave academia and to consult as a counselor, mediator and social psychologist. She still teaches at UCSC on occasion. She believes in treating the human body with respect, which includes nourishing it with good nutrition and daily exercise. She continues to publish her applied research on human rights and truth commissions and believes world peace is possible in our time. Connect with Cath at www.CathByrne.com.

Tina and Séamus Murphy

○ ★ ○

WHAT DO YOU REALLY WANT?

Tina!
Love Life &
Live Your
Dream!

We first saw each other at the end of a seminar in January, 2006. We held each other's gaze for a few seconds, looked away, and when we looked back, the other was gone. In that fleeting moment, we both felt an instant spark, a thread of curiosity, an attractive connection.

Ten months later, at four a.m. on Saturday, October 7, 2006, I'm riding from southern to northern California with my friends Cherie and Harold, on our way to a leadership conference. I finally broke up with my boyfriend of two-and-a-half years last night. It was a difficult decision, but the right one for me.

I know I deserve better; I deserve to be in a happy, honest, loving, trusting and fulfilling relationship. So when will I find someone who truly loves me for who I am?

As we cruise along the highway in the pale blue pre-dawn light, Harold at the wheel, Cherie beside him, and me in the back, I take out my yellow legal pad and write the date and my name at the top: "Tina." Below that, I write, "What do I want in a #10 relationship with the man of my dreams?" As I think about all the relationships I've had and my past divorces, I turn over the big questions that have been brewing in my mind: *What do I want more of in my life? How do I want to be treated? What do I enjoy? How do I want him to be with my family? What kind of man will I be happy with for the rest of my life?*

I start to make a positive, detailed list of answers to these questions, stating only what I want, not what I don't want:

- Available legally, emotionally, spiritually and geographically.
- Grounded.
- Smiles easily.
- Takes the time just to tell me he loves me and is thinking of me.
- Has a great sense of humor.
- Loves to see me smile and be happy.
- Adores and respects me for who I am and how I look.

Throughout the long drive, I alternate between writing and dozing. As the list grows, I feel more certain and more at ease.

When I think my list is complete, I share it with Cherie. "Which items would you say are non-negotiable?" she asks.

What a great question—which of these things must the man of my dreams possess? Which, if missing, will tell me not to pursue a relationship with this man? I mark each of these

When will I find someone who truly loves me for who I am?

characteristics and qualities with a star. I end up with thirty-nine non-negotiable items, and very few items on the list are not starred. I feel such a sense of excitement—I am sure I'll get what I want, what I deserve!

We are both surprised to see each other again, sharing a van from our hotel to the conference. *Wow, it's that beautiful Hawaiian woman!* I flash back to that moment at the seminar ten months earlier and say to her, "You look familiar."

She smiles at me and says, "You're from Honolulu." Then she reads my nametag: "Séamus F. Murphy, Honolulu, Hawaii."

From the first moment, the energy and attraction I feel are remarkable. Over dinner together that evening, Tina and I spend a lot of time talking. I feel so comfortable with her—which is amazing, given we just met! In the past, I've often been intimidated by beautiful women. But Tina is different.

A mutual friend mentions to me that she believes Tina is in a relationship.

"That's okay," I say. "I just really like this woman for who she is, and I want to continue to get to know her."

On day three of the conference, single participants are given red hearts to put on their nametags, and when I see Tina at lunch, she's wearing one—she's available! My heart leaps.

"I've just broken up with someone," she confides to me. "This time I'm doing things differently. On my way up here, I made a list of everything I want in a relationship. Would you like to read a little of it?"

Hah! She's got a list too? She really is *the perfect woman.* About a year before, I did the exact same thing. I'd been married twice. and when a friend asked me, "What do you want in a relationship? How do you want to feel? What are the traits and qualities you're looking for in a woman?" I responded by sitting down at the computer and creating a list divided into five different quadrants, all connected: emotional, physical, spiritual, practical and recreational. I wrote down all the ways I hoped to communicate with the woman of my dreams, the things I hoped we'd do together. My friend encouraged me to refine the list, and it grew more detailed over the weeks.

When it was finished, I was filled with excitement. I kept thinking: *What am I doing? Will I be laughed at? Is this real? What if I get what I want?*

I knew I wouldn't get what I wanted if I didn't let others know, so I decided to put it out to the universe in every possible way. I sent my list as an e-mail to all my contacts, everyone I knew.

I felt a huge sense of relief once I hit the "SEND" button. It was out there, all right!

Now here she is, sitting right next to me: the woman of my dreams. Each day, Tina reads me a short section of her list, teasing me a little, testing the waters as we laugh, joke, talk and share stories. I feel such excitement; I'm like a teenager again!

On day five of the conference, sitting outside at lunch under the shade of an oak tree, with the sun shining on us through its leaves, Tina lets me read her entire list. It's as though she's

*How wonderful to end up with
the partner of our dreams!*

opened up her whole heart for me to see, and I see myself as her dream man. Of her thirty-nine non-negotiable items, there's only one I don't match: the annual income. I point at it. "I'm retired from the Navy and love my job as a sailing instructor. I'm pretty close, but don't make that much."

"I'm confident you will," she says. "Besides, it's not my highest priority. This list is you all over!"

The singles event organized for today is about to begin. I look into Tina's gorgeous green eyes and say, "You know, I don't want to do this. I feel comfortable with you."

She snuggles up beside me, takes my hand and says, "I feel the same way." We both decide to skip the event and head to the port-a-potties instead. Nervous and happy, I pull the little red heart off my nametag and toss it in the trash. When I emerge, I see Tina coming out of a neighboring potty. The little red heart has disappeared from her nametag, too. We smile and take each other's hand. And then we walk back into the conference, together. And we've been together ever since. How wonderful to end up with the partner of our dreams!

We often laugh at the thought that if we had only dated, it would have taken us months to get to know each other, versus that one magical week in October, 2006. We've since grown to love and adore each other deeply, and we use open communication and heartfelt connection to continually enhance our relationship. In each other, we find true acceptance and love for who we are.

Séamus surprised me with his marriage proposal on July 20, 2007 at the Honolulu Airport before we flew out to an entrepreneur workshop. After hurrying through the check-in process, we ordered dinner and drinks to relax. Then he said, "So, do you want to get married?"

I couldn't believe what I was hearing and asked, "What did you say?"

He repeated, "Do you want to get married?" Although he didn't have a ring at that time, he quickly picked up an onion ring from my dinner plate and used that instead.

Tears streamed down my face as I replied, "Yes!" and happily accepted his ring. We were married on June 29, 2008, with my oldest son, Colton, giving me away and my other two children, Ethan and Arielle, at my side.

People love to hear our story. Our single friends are always asking us what they can do to have what we have. The first question we ask them is, "Do you have a list?" Many of them have lists—in their heads—that change depending on who they

So... what do you want?

meet. We encourage them to write down exactly what they want because the more specific they are, the more likely it is that they will attract that relationship into their lives.

So... what do you want? Speak and write about the positive attributes and feelings that you want to experience and enjoy. You can learn from your past experiences what you *don't* want— great. However, what do you *really* want?

How do you want to feel in a relationship? What experiences do you want to create together? What are the feelings you're going to have together and when you're apart? Imagine what it's like when you're holding hands with this person—how does it feel? How are you going to be when you're with this person? Get in touch with the sensation of being with the man or woman of your dreams. Be present with it. Bring it from waaayyy out there to how it feels now, in the present moment. Wow—what an amazing feeling!

Entrepreneurs and partners in love, Tina Murphy (President of Rapport Innovations, Inc.) and Séamus Murphy (President of Starboardguy Productions, Inc.) created a relationship game based on their lists called "What do you want?—the inspiring game of connections." The game inspires others to write a list and attract (or appreciate) the partner of their dreams, just as Tina and Séamus did.

Shortly after the couple married on June 29, 2008, Séamus published his first book: Sailing with Mr. Séamus; Pull the Tiller Towards You, *in which he shares his passion for teaching kids how to sail. He is currently at work on his second book. To learn more, visit www.SailingWithMrSeamus.com. Find the game and connect with the Murphys at www.WhatDoYouWantGame.com.*

Edward T. Coda

○ ⭐ ○

THE HOUSE OUR DREAM BUILT

How could we go on strike and lose even more money? It seemed crazy. I was so frustrated and discouraged, I just wanted to bang my head against my desk.

I had changed careers to teach accounting in the university system, and the pay was horrible. Betty and I had racked up huge, seemingly insurmountable credit-card debt and were robbing Peter to pay Paul every month—not to mention the fact that our six children all needed to eat. As the breadwinner in our large, happy family, I was completely overwhelmed.

In my office after—ironically—teaching a class on inflation accounting, I saw the posting on my door: the union recommended striking because we weren't getting a two-percent pay increase. I plugged my university salary for the past nine years into the inflation chart and realized in horror that we were striking and still stood to lose yet more money. We weren't keeping up with inflation ourselves, and here we were, the premier institution in the state! I threw up my hands and said aloud, "I can't do this anymore."

In just six months I would qualify for a state pension. However, I knew that, if I stayed at the university, not only would I continue to go deeper into debt, but also I would keep dragging my feet and never commit to my dream of full-time financial planning.

I had tremendous fear about making the leap. All six of our kids were still living at home. *What if I don't make it? I have all this responsibility; am I crazy?*

Betty agreed to take a teaching position for two years to give us some security, so I could get the business started. Scary as it was, we knew the potential of making this transition. And we were really doing it together.

For the first time, I faced the fact that we needed to create financial abundance in order to fulfill some of our dreams. I'd

As the breadwinner in our large, happy family, I was completely overwhelmed.

always had negative attitudes about money, ingrained from my childhood, like: *If you have too much money, it's harder to get into heaven.* It was partly a worth issue: *You don't deserve it and can't have it.* And, it was also a guilt issue: *It'll be bad for you. It'll go to your head or make you greedy if you do get it.* I knew in my heart and soul that I just wanted to educate and help people with their money. It never occurred to me that it was okay for me to have money, too. But, when I started looking at all my goals and wishes and hopes for the family, some of them did require money: like creating a house in which each of the kids could have the privacy and sacred space of his or her own room.

At first, I woke up feeling unemployed and worrying about whether I had made the right choice. I was totally stressed and had anxiety attacks and never-ending colds. I felt a constant insecurity and fear in my gut. I would laugh and have fun with the family, but always with that nagging thought: *Am I good enough?*

It took almost a year before I even started to feel encouraged. Things really took off when Betty and I started to meet weekly with some friends who'd gone to a PSI World Seminars weekend. They shared the total positive attitude we believed in, and we were inspired by them and the concepts they got from PSI of setting a vision, making goals and dreaming big. They involved us in their Mastermind group, and I began to actively reprogram my thinking. We started believing "we can make this happen" instead of just hoping it would.

In December of 1987, we had a big family meeting in the nine-hundred-square-foot, three-bedroom home where the eight of us were "living." Betty and I wanted to start to dream big together as a family, so we taped lengths of butcher paper to the walls and got out a bunch of colored markers. Each of us called out our individual and family goals and dreams, which we wrote on the butcher paper in bright colors. I can still feel the churn of excitement and enthusiasm that emerged as we put those dreams up for all of us to see.

We wrote down everything, even the wildest stuff. I dreamed of a job where I could be present at all the kids' events, including coaching their baseball teams. Betty and I dreamed of every kid being able to go to college. We also dreamed of a family that would

We needed to create financial abundance
in order to fulfill some of our dreams.

be close and remain close no matter where the kids went to school or chose to live after college.

We summarized our greatest dream this way: "To live a passionate love affair with our God, with each other as a couple, with our children and in our business, so that others will be attracted to want what we have and know they can have it by seeing us live it!"

These were all beautiful long-term goals, but the most pressing goal was a bigger house. Somebody threw it out right away: "I want my own bedroom!"

Others piped, "Yes! And I want my own bathroom." We all worked together to draw a picture of our dream house on the paper.

Our oldest, Jennifer, always our reality check, rolled her eyes. "Great. Another pipe dream. I'm sure I'll be long gone before any of this happens."

But Jennifer was wrong. Working on weekends, building slowly in parallel with our financial planning business, we expanded and added onto our home. And within just two years of doing our butcher-paper dreaming, we had turned our cramped little house into a six-bedroom, four-bathroom, almost-four-thousand-square-foot mansion with a sunken living room! The transformation was just unbelievable, and to create it almost two whole years before Jennifer went off to college was a miracle. She got her own room and a bathroom.

You can have anything—you just have to
get clear about money so you can create it.

I felt immense pride and joy as we shared our accomplishment with all our family and friends on the day of our housewarming, but the best moment may have been on that first night, when we put a ladder up to the roof and all eight of us climbed up. We lay side by side on a blanket, looking out at the vast beauty of the night sky and all its shooting stars. As I listened to the sounds of awe and wonder coming from the mouths of our children, I could not hold back my happy tears. Look what we were able to create together!

I wanted to be an example to show our kids that anything in their lives would be possible, and I was. The house was the big goal, the beautiful thing we all dreamed up together. Having it come true meant I really delivered.

After Betty and I finally attended a PSI weekend in 2002, I knew why everything our friends had shared with us had become reality. I stopped worrying about whether we could make it or not and got it that we could do anything we chose to do. These days I live with an assurance that we are always putting our dreams into motion. And I've really come to believe that God helps those who help themselves. Prayer really works, and putting things out that we really want is okay. It doesn't have to be only what we need. You can have anything—you just have to get clear about money so you can create it.

Fast-forward to today: We now have our own independent financial-planning business. Four of our six children and two of their spouses work side by side with Betty and me every day. Some people think we are crazy to want to be together all the time, but that was our dream when we were dating and talking about getting married, and now it has become a dream come true. We have offices in Hawaii and North Carolina and are continually looking to expand. Not only do our associate representatives and employees become "family," all of our clients do, too.

We once stifled our growth—and ability to spread our message—by putting personal financial wealth on the back burner. We just didn't do for ourselves what we did for other people. I know we would be so much farther along in our journey if we had done that sooner, instead of remaining controlled and stuck in our old belief systems.

Now we are focused on creating abundant wealth so that we can spread the message of what we have created to the whole world and help others in the way we always dreamed. I want to shout to the world that it is so much simpler and easier to go for creating abundance from the beginning.

We still have the butcher paper from that fateful family meeting in December of 1987, and we often think of that day to remind us just how powerful and possible it is to make our dreams come true. In fact, every year after, while we lived together in that house, we created new visions, wrote down all of our hopes and dreams and referred to our colorful notes the next year to see how far we each had come.

Money is a tool to help you get where you want to go. Start dreaming now, but don't waste time trying to do it alone. Surround yourself with like-minded, enthusiastic and affirming friends and family who will relish sharing your success.

Gather your loved ones and draw up the plans for your own "dream house," whether it is a real house or a different adventure. Write it on poster board. Paint your wall with chalkboard paint and scribble it in primary colors. Draw it on a piece of paper and post copies in every room in your house. Imagine the dream *together*, and then, *together*, create the dream. It's as simple as dream, pray and go!

Edward T. Coda, CFP, MBA, acts as Coda Financial Group's Senior Vice President and General Agent. He has over forty years' experience in the finance industry, including work as a CPA with Ernst and Ernst; as a tenured instructor in accounting with the University of Hawaii system; and buying, building, running and selling his own business. Ed is blessed to be working with his family on a daily basis, and he loves helping clients achieve their life goals while feeling secure in their choices. He has worked tirelessly to teach financial literacy and help people understand that money can be a positive, powerful tool to enhance relationships and lifestyle. Ed and his wife Betty co-authored the bestselling Passionate Parent, Passionate Couple, *a book that gives valuable tools and humorous insight into building permanent marriages and strong families. You can connect with Ed at www.PassionateParentCouple.com and www. CodaFinancialGroup.com.*

Securities and advisory services offered through National Planning Corporation (NPC), Member FINRA/SIPC, a Registered Investment Adviser. Coda Financial Group, Inc. and NPC are separate and unrelated companies.

Shirley A. Hunt

○ ★ ○

DARE TO DREAM

Every night, as the sky darkened from twilight to a deep city blue, I sat on my next-door neighbors' garage roof and watched the stars come out. As I drew my own maps of the constellations and wished on falling stars, I dreamed of a life beyond Grafton Hill. *I'm going to get out of this place. And I'm going to get Mom and Herb and Lila out of here, too.*

The world out there was so big—it called to me. There had to be more to life than sitting here, on this one tiny point on the earth, watching life struggle on around me in poverty and limitation. I wanted to travel and meet different people. *Most of all,* I thought, *I want to make a lot of money, so we don't have to worry anymore. I can buy Mom and Dad a nice house in a nice neighborhood with big trees... send my sister to college...*

In the 1950s, when I was a kid, Grafton Hill was a Christian-Lebanese ghetto in Worcester, Massachusetts. The community was tight-knit to the point of separation from the rest of the world, almost as if the adults were trying to recreate Lebanon in the United States. I never saw a blond person until I went to school; when I did, I ran home and told my father excitedly, "I saw a person with hair the color of a broom!"

My siblings—Herb and Lila—and I were first-generation Lebanese-Americans, and we had two great examples in our parents. They embodied integrity, honesty and love, and let nothing stand in their way when they came to a strange, new land to build a better life. My father didn't speak English, but that didn't stop him from finding work and making a home for us. My mother was a very small person, standing just under four feet tall, but she didn't let that stop her, either. When people stared at her, even taunted her for being so tiny (and, in some places, for being dark), she just ignored them and went about her business. She was tough. I admired her spirit.

We were very poor, and things got worse
after my father died when I was sixteen.

Most of the other Lebanese women I grew up around were completely subservient to men and spent most of their time in the kitchen, cooking for their men, or waiting on them hand and foot. They also cleaned and crocheted, but didn't seem to do much else. All my female cousins were married with children by the time they were sixteen or seventeen years old, and most of them ended up in abusive relationships.

I didn't see many examples of lives I wanted to emulate, if any. And, I lacked self-confidence. Singled out in school because of my "exotic" looks and habits, I always thought I was less than everybody else. But that didn't stop me from stargazing and dreaming of a life of freedom, adventure and wealth.

As I said, Grafton Hill was a ghetto. My family scraped by, and there was a lot of love in our home to keep us going; but we were very poor, and things got worse after my father died when I was sixteen.

The Thanksgiving after he died, the Salvation Army brought us dinner. I looked at the stiff, pitying smile on the face of the volunteer who held out the turkey and suddenly realized just how poor we had become. Nothing I'd been dreaming about would just magically come true—making a different life would be up to me. I felt a deep sense of responsibility. I had to do all I could to help my mother and fill the void and all the need left by my father's death. I decided: *It is up to me to make sure my sister gets a college education. It is up to me to make sure we have food on the table. It is up to me to get my family out of here.*

I did not know how I would make it happen. How would I get the education or the self-confidence I needed? What if I never could amount to anything special in this world after all? I yearned to save us all from the ghetto with every fiber of my being.

Sitting on my rooftop perch, I pictured all of us living in a beautiful house, my mother being able to buy whatever she wanted and the whole family traveling to exotic places and staying in fancy hotels. I often missed my father the most when he showed up in these dreams but—of course—was not there when I went back in the house.

At sixteen, it seemed clear to me that my family needed money more than I needed a diploma. I dropped out of high school. One of my teachers really believed in me, really cared about me. He

I had worked my way out of the ghetto, but when would I really find success?

hounded me to get my GED. When I told him I thought night school would be a waste of time, he said, "Then I'm sending you to secretarial school." So I enrolled in secretarial school and got a job.

And this is where life works its magic! One evening, at the secretarial school, a lovely young woman offered to give me a ride home. I told her, "You don't want to go where I live."

She wondered why.

I told her I lived in Grafton Hill, and she said, "That's true. I'm not supposed to go there."

But she did take me home—to the wrong side of the tracks— because that's the kind of girl Jane Willhite always was, even then. That evening's conversation in her car marked the beginning of a fifty-five-year-long friendship, in many ways the most significant of my life.

By that time I had been a member of the workforce for years and was the single mother of a six-year-old daughter, Jane had started a company called the Personal Success Institute (PSI). It offered personal growth seminars, but I never found the time to attend one. I had already achieved the wealth and financial independence I planned for as a child and strived for as an adult. However, from

It was time to share more with the world, time to expand my notion of my purpose in life.

what I knew of Jane and her vision, I sensed that her work would be a way to make my life better, bigger, fuller and more spiritual. I wanted all of that; I had worked my way out of the ghetto, but when would I really find success?

I decided to enroll. During the seminar, I had a kind of awakening. I learned more about myself in several days than I felt I'd been aware of all my life. I still dreamed all the time—and discovered that I usually convinced myself to stop short of realizing my biggest dreams because I still felt somehow "less than." Jane and PSI World Seminars helped me to see that if I just got out of my own way, I could make the dreams I'd always cherished for my family come true.

By 1977, I had achieved the wealth I dreamed of as a child. One of the ten highest-earning saleswomen in my field, I was living the "good life" of the nouveau riche: lots of parties, international travel. I got everyone out of the ghetto on Grafton Hill, bought a house and cars for my mother and sister and gave whatever I could to help my extended family, too. I traveled with my young daughter, Shellie, and expanded her world as much as possible. Life was looking as I'd dreamed it would from that rooftop in the ghetto.

But then I hit a bit of a wall. One day I bought a very elegant, expensive chandelier, and when I brought it home, I thought, *This is not where it's at. Life is not just about making money.* Because I had spent so much of my life dreaming, it had become a habit; and now I dreamed of bigger and better things.

I realized then that my career needed to change. Something in me wanted to follow my deeper dream of helping other people. Just succeeding on my own, even though I could take good care of my family, was not enough. I remembered the PSI seminar, and concepts that kept coming back to me: "Givers gain;" "Win-win."

It was time to share more with the world, time to expand my notion of my purpose in life. I decided to go and visit my dear friend Jane in California. So I packed my little girl and went to spend a couple of months with Jane and her husband.

That was thirty-five years ago, and the beginning of a beautiful collaboration with Jane, working at PSI and discovering the real dream beneath my dream of riches: the dream of sharing true wealth.

Since then, I've had the joy of helping to transform the lives of over half a million dreamers who have come to PSI, many from ghettos of shame, poverty, illness, bad marriages and other hardships, all seeking more for themselves—sometimes more money, sure—but also more wisdom, more power, more joy and more self-knowledge and awareness.

These fellow stargazers of mine have shared so many stories of fulfillment and transformation, it's impossible for me to pick just one to tell you about. Suffice it to say, I have seen half a million examples (including my own) of this truth: No matter the obstacle, no matter the physical, mental or emotional ghetto you may have lived in or are living in right now, you, too, have the power to create the life you dream about—to reach up and touch that star that speaks to you.

Shirley A. Hunt is President of PSI Seminars. The daughter of Lebanese immigrants, she soared from the ghetto to become one of the ten highest-paid saleswomen in her field. She joined the PSI team in 1977 and has coached and mentored over half a million people since. Her focus is on continuing the business of hope for the next generation. Connect with Shirley at www. PSIWorldSeminars.com.

Kevin M. Jennings

○ ✪ ○

TABLE FOR SEVEN

Words poured out of me from I knew not where. Tears welled up as I drafted words that spoke of accomplishments I had never before imagined, and had certainly not done.

I had spent twenty years in the high-tech industry, which, though it paid very well, was not personally fulfilling. I was burnt out. I needed to feel that I was contributing to the world in a meaningful way. But I could see no way to use what I thought of as my limited capabilities to make an important contribution.

PSI World Seminars helped me see that I had created those limitations myself. Now I was finishing a ninety-day goal-setting and goal-accomplishing "game" called Pacesetter Leadership Dynamics (PLD), in which one of my main goals was to determine what I would do next, now that I'd left the high-tech sector. Eighty-nine days had passed, and I was no closer to that goal. Now that I had the confidence to tackle most anything, I was frustrated because I had no idea what that thing might be. I still had not made any noticeable, tangible progress in discovering my next career; I despaired of coming up with something that would make a difference to the world.

On the last day of the PLD course, our team of fifteen met amid the majestic trees, gleaming sunshine and picturesque vistas of a beautiful northern California ranch. We were given this challenge:

Imagine that it is your one-hundredth birthday. Tell your team what you have accomplished in your life. I went outside to face what seemed an insurmountable challenge. And I began to write words that emanated from a source I cannot to this day explain. It seemed that someone else was writing with my hand. I had no time for worries about what I couldn't do, wasn't worthy of doing.

I wrote that I had been an instrument in saving many, many people—perhaps millions—from starvation. I had started a chain of restaurants where, when a patron ordered an entrée, a meal

Everyone gets a seat at the table—everyone gets to eat!

was purchased for a starving person. Diners would enjoy the abundance of a delicious restaurant meal all the more knowing that, somewhere in the world, a desperately hungry person was also enjoying a nutritious meal. I had grown this concept into a chain of hundreds of locations and had, in the process, fed millions of meals to starving people throughout the world.

As I delivered this speech to my fellow teammates, with the conviction that I had actually created my chain of restaurants, I had to focus intently on my words and speak in a deliberate and paced manner in order not to break down into tears. When I saw how positively my audience received my idea, I got a chill. *Wow, this is real. This could have a big impact, not because I have ingenuity, but because it resonates. People want to eat at a restaurant that does this; they want to take part, to be involved somehow.* I knew I had found what I would next do with my life.

The next morning was my fiftieth birthday. My first thought was of my idea. I knew I had reached a watershed. As my wife and I stood in the security-check line at the airport, I realized that I had emotionally bonded to my new life path. I was walking in a new direction, on cloud nine. For the first time in a very long time, I felt satisfied, confident, serene. My wife saw the change in me, and smiled her approval.

Before long, I realized that it would take many decades, under the best of circumstances, to build a chain of restaurants. And I learned that, every day, fifteen-thousand people die of starvation. Starving people couldn't wait years. Instead, I would work with existing restaurants so that when a patron ordered a meal, it would result in someone else in the world being fed. My inspiration incarnated as "Table for Seven," a company dedicated to fundamentally transforming the restaurant industry so that it becomes commonplace for a person's entrée order to trigger the purchase and distribution of a meal to someone, somewhere in the world, who would otherwise go hungry and perhaps starve.

Table for Seven refers to the seven continents, and the vision is that everyone gets a seat at the table—everyone gets to eat! Table for Seven, working with restaurants that participate in the Table for Seven Alliance, expects to be feeding one-million hungry people every day by 2016. Given the millions and millions of restaurant

I want more. I want to be thrilled,
captivated by what I do. I deserve it.

meals served each day, it's an achievable goal, and a new way to tackle the problem of world hunger. People eat in restaurants to enjoy good food with friends and family. They don't want to brood about starving children. Table for Seven encourages them to savor their meals even more, knowing that they have saved a life with each entrée they've ordered. And, since their dining experience was better than usual, they'll come back again and again, and participating restaurants will thrive and prosper.

Naturally, within a couple of days, my doubts arose. They still do. *You know nothing about the restaurant business, or about international philanthropy. You've never run a business. Who are you to think you can take on a project of this magnitude? Restaurateurs will have to pay for the free meals. How will you convince them to participate?* I spin my wheels sometimes, but then I remember all the people I've told about Table for Seven, who keep asking about it and to whom I am accountable. I don't know exactly how I'll do it, but I know I will. At other times, I tell myself that I'll consider those negatives next week.

For now, I keep in mind that, though if it's to be it's up to me, some things are up to the universe to provide. I don't need all the skills required to achieve my dream. I can hire talented experts, and I believe the right people will appear at the right time as I network and continue forward.

I owe Table for Seven the courtesy of doing my due diligence and equipping myself, so I am going to business school to get training. After all, when I present this idea to a chain of restaurants that will cost them a lot of money, and try to convince them that the

---

*We are all capable of doing enormous
things. Our only limitations are
those we place on ourselves.*

---

program will more than compensate by filling additional seats—an unproven concept—I need to have my ducks in a row. I know that I face many challenges. But the strength of the idea, and its value, trump everything else.

We're never given a dream that we're not empowered to realize. My own personal experience, along with a lot of observation, has shown me how we self-select ourselves out of greatness. We tell ourselves, "That would never work for me. I'm just not up to it." That's why an ordinary person, with a positive attitude and an openness to the idea of accomplishing something great, so often achieves more than brilliant people who believe in their limitations.

Most of us settle for a vocation that we're not thrilled about. We're willing to put up with it because we've already convinced ourselves we don't have other options. It doesn't have to be that way. We aren't put here to endure spending most of our waking hours doing what we don't love.

I want more. I want to be thrilled, captivated by what I do. I deserve it. If you're not thrilled and captivated every day by your work, your surroundings, your relationships, then it's up to you to change them. Be brutally honest with yourself, now. Are you where you deserve to be? If not, it's time to open yourself to finding what will take advantage of your deeper longings. When I wrote that speech, my goal seemed to come from nowhere. My wife and I had done some work with the Nourish the Children organization, which is dedicated to alleviating hunger; yet, as I sought to figure out what next to do with my life, saving starving people was certainly not at the forefront of my mind. And I had no connection with the restaurant business, beyond eating in restaurants as a patron. Your deepest purpose may be far from your conscious awareness.

We are all capable of doing enormous things. Our only limitations are those we place on ourselves. We are each here for a purpose, and if we are intent on discovering what it is, it will come. It may seemingly emerge out of nowhere. If you want a vision of something more, commit to finding out what it is. This will take deliberate effort. Expect your vision to come—even if the journey of discovery appears to be hopeless—and embrace it when it arrives.

So now it's your turn: Imagine that it is your one-hundredth birthday. Tell me: What have you accomplished in your life?

Kevin Jennings has a hunger for one thing: to eradicate world hunger! He founded Table for Seven, a nonprofit organization dedicated to addressing the problem of widespread starvation. "Seven" refers to the seven continents, and the idea is setting a table big enough for everyone to have a seat—everyone gets to eat! Each time a patron orders an entrée at a participating restaurant, a matching, nutritionally sound meal will be fed to someone who might otherwise starve. Table for Seven's "Drink Well" program will also allocate one cent from each beverage purchase toward fresh water programs. Table for Seven is in its startup phase, with a goal of feeding over one million people every day by 2016.

Kevin spent over twenty years in the high-technology industry, providing computer-networking solutions to large corporations and educational institutions. He is currently studying for an MBA at the prestigious Thunderbird School of Global Management in Glendale, Arizona. This will equip him with the skills to propel Table for Seven into a global organization that seamlessly leverages something we commonly do—dine in a restaurant— into a game-changing mechanism that addresses the problem of world hunger. Connect with Kevin at www.TableForSeven.com.

Roswitha Shanahan, PsyD

○ ★ ○

BECOME YOUR OWN HERO

NUCLEAR NIGHTMARE, the headlines said. *2,000 DEAD IN ATOM HORROR.*

It was April, 1987, and I was eight months pregnant with my second child. My husband and I were living in Turkey at the time and we watched in terror as the Chernobyl disaster and the devastating effects of its radiation continued to monopolize the front pages of newspapers and almost every television news show, even a year after the disaster occurred.

As my due date grew closer and photographs began to emerge of babies in the region, born with horrific deformities, concern for our unborn child only grew. When I was in the hospital, other mothers told me that the hospitals were full of babies with birth defects because of the Chernobyl disaster. Every mother lamented what had happened to our kids. The doctors were unable to tell me whether my baby would be born healthy or not. I was confronted with the possibility the baby would not be born healthy, even though I didn't want to take it in or let it be real in my mind.

In May, my worst fears were confirmed. Nicole, our second daughter, was born with an omphalocele. In babies with an omphalocele, the intestines are covered only by a thin layer of tissue and can be seen easily. The first time I saw Nicole, it looked like she had a big apple hanging on her belly, with just a membrane-thin layer of skin holding it in place. I felt my heart sink and shatter, and despite the effects of the Chernobyl disaster, I couldn't help but blame myself. *Did I do or eat something wrong? Did I stretch too much? What did I do to cause this?*

I yearned for some clarity to sweep away the confusion that ate at me. The Turkish doctors gave Nicole a fifty/fifty chance of surviving the surgery she desperately needed, and when I heard those statistics, my first instinct was to take her to Germany, where

I was confronted with the possibility the baby would not be born healthy.

I grew up. We would risk her life by taking her out of the country; she was so young, and riddled with an infection that could only be treated with a topical antiseptic.

My husband and I had to make the decision: not to survive the trip to Germany, or not to survive the surgery in Turkey. We had applied for a passport for Nicole when we were first told diagnosis and treatment options. When it arrived, on Nicole's sixth day of life, we decided to take the plunge and fly back to Germany.

The flight seemed to take forever, and all I could keep telling myself—as I had been doing since her diagnosis—was that my beautiful baby girl was going to be okay, even though the odds were stacked against her. She had to be.

When we reached Germany, the general physician said it was a miracle that she was still alive. When I heard those words, it was as though a small ray of light shone into the dark spaces of my mind taken up with constant stress and sickening worry for my fragile little girl. She had such a long way to go; yet she was already a miracle. We immediately took her to the hospital, and were told by the doctors that because her infection was so bad, they could not operate on her. She was kept in the hospital to ensure that the infection went down, but after three weeks of trying everything they could think of, all they could tell me to do was, "Keep her clean and she will get better."

Every morning, afternoon and evening, I bathed her in chamomile, which helped to release the infection. My hands shook and I blinked back heavy tears, only able to take comfort in the words of my father, who always reassured me that she would be okay, and that I shouldn't worry. I kept those words with me every minute of every hour of every day, even when my own strength of spirit was fading.

Before long, it was Nicole who was turning my life around. Even in the hospital, where she must have been in so much pain, and so tired from struggling on, she never cried. She only looked at me, as if reassuring me that things were going to be okay.

When I looked at her, took her in, I just surrendered to her divine presence—her gaze was what made me most aware of the divine presence in a baby. I felt exhilarated simply by the light of who she was. She was so much more, in the source of her divine being, than I ever was. In her peaceful, gentle way, she helped me

---

I could only exist in the now.

---

to release the suffering of my preoccupation—her possible death—that always loomed like a shadowy monster in the corner of my mind's eye. I realized that the loving being within her was within me also: an inner fountain of strength that I could drink from.

When I surrendered to her, I totally let go of the fear. I said, "God, you are in her. I am letting go of all my fears and worries and self-blame." I felt such relief and just let her be. I gave myself over completely to the reality of the moment, and let myself be in the moment rather than worry about the future, knowing that the future could not be changed. I could only exist in the now. It felt like a gift.

I used to resist the quiet. It was difficult for me to let myself just sit and grow calm, when it seemed there were always better things to do, and more productive ways to spend my time. But what could possibly be better, or more productive, than pouring my heart and soul into caring for my baby? And in doing that, I couldn't help but let go of my own battles. How could I be so indulgent as to wage my own internal wars when Nicole's were so much more important?

I finally realized that, even though I was suffering, I needed to open my heart. How could I feel love and goodness if I remained closed off, wrapped up in my own worry? I decided to just sit in the stillness and breathe and not give any more attention to worrying, for I understood that love is the most important relationship. My inner feelings of who I am became so expansive! I felt a level of love, understanding and appreciation I had never experienced before.

I felt a level of love, understanding and appreciation I had never experienced before.

Nicole inspired me to create more good in my life. Instead of holding on to what I didn't want, I opened up to what I yearned for. Through these experiences, I realized that fear was holding me back from my true and loving self. My inner being, the source within me, was expanded, and felt love and appreciation for me. When I felt worried, fearful, I didn't love, but instead separated from myself and from others. Every time I found fault with something or someone, I separated myself from my inner source, my inner power. I realized that I was born to honor and respect my body, mind and soul, and to surrender to the peace within.

Months passed, and Nicole's infection steadily got better so that, by November, she could travel with us to Hawaii. In February, we went to Germany for my father's funeral and Nicole had her surgery there.

In May, she finally had her operation. They fixed her completely. I will always remember how all the doctors and nurses said she was a miracle child, and that they were amazed by how strong her will was. It was divine to see such a small baby with her will and strength to survive. Of course, that wasn't the end of the fight. On and off, as Nicole grew up, other complications arose. She developed scoliosis, but managed to handle it without any problems thanks to her indomitable spirit.

Nicole knows the story behind her scar, where the doctors created a belly button for her, as well. When the cruel children at school used to tease her, calling her a turkey, she came home crying. She only ever felt comfortable wearing a swimsuit, not a bikini. So I told her to be proud of her scar, because it showed how strong she was; she had strength nobody else had. Nicole was born into the curse of hitting the ground running—of being in the biggest fight of her life before her life had even begun—and she triumphed.

I told her that she was a miracle baby, and when she realized her own spirit and divinity, she started to see herself in a different light. She became less afraid to show her scar, recognizing it was a scar that came from a miracle. And when I sent her my story, she was so happy and so amazed to have done what she did for me without even knowing it. Nicole finally saw herself as I had seen her for so long: She became her own hero.

When you are calm, and feel the presence of light and divinity, you create a magical inner joy because you can allow yourself to come from your heart and connect with an inner awareness, an inner space. You can allow yourself to be quiet, and to have no interferences.

The vision I have for my life is more clear and powerful without all the noise. When obstacles and challenges arise, I acknowledge that I need to breathe and not create a drama in my mind: It's the thought that creates the acts that follow. So I keep still, wait and surrender to the knowledge that what I need to do will become clear.

What could you achieve if you let yourself be still? Could you become your own hero?

Roswitha Shanahan, PsyD, is a licensed clinical psychologist and a Kundalini Yoga teacher. She received her doctorate in psychology from the American School of Professional Psychology, is certified in eye movement desensitization (EMDR) and hypnotherapy, and has received extensive training in emotional field therapy, play therapy and progressive relaxation techniques. She uses her skills and experience to help people create their best life, and to recognize their own innate light and divinity.

David Reinsma

WILLING TO
RISK IT ALL

Part of me was dying, and I knew why. For ten years I had poured my heart and soul into an environmental consulting firm. One other geologist, a chemical engineer and I were minority partners. We had met our goal of turning the business into a larger and more profitable firm. George, the majority partner, rarely even visited the business. Each year, when it was time to share the profits according to our contract, George had reasons why the division couldn't happen.

I believed that George was sucking the lifeblood out of the company, and that we would never reach our potential with the lack of leadership, integrity and honesty he showed in his business dealings with us, his own partners.

I was undervalued at work, and my personal life wasn't any better. My wife had asked for a separation and the divorce papers had been filed. We shared custody of our three children. My soon-to-be-ex-wife had been a stay-at-home mom for many years, so the financial burden was on my shoulders. My life was in turmoil because of my divorce, and financially things were looking much worse for me than they had looked in a long time. I was paying for two homes. To save money, I had moved in with friends who had three children. But they had problems of their own and could not offer the companionship and support I so desperately needed.

I knew that, if I confronted George, I might very well be fired. *What if I lose my house? What if I'm not able to support my kids? What if I don't find another job?* I had every reason in the world to just bite my lip, shut my mouth and keep quiet. But deep down I knew that, if I gave up on what I believed, I would never realize my dream of owning a company that lived by the foundational principles of hard work, honesty and integrity.

After I silenced my fears and grounded myself in what I really wanted for my life, I called George and asked him to set some time

I was undervalued at work, and my personal life wasn't any better.

aside for a meeting. It had been four years since we'd met one-on-one. George was a master of delay and put off meeting after meeting. Each delay was an obstacle, an excuse to just put my nose back to the grindstone and let the injustice continue. But I was determined. I had not realized the monetary fruits of my labors, despite bumper financial crops most years; nor was I acknowledged for my contribution, or valued for my skills.

I had all my ducks in a row when we finally met. The tension in my office when George came in and sat down was like wind you can't see, but know is there from the movement of the hairs on the back of your neck or across your forearm. The small talk lasted only a moment.

George quickly asked what it was that I wanted to talk to him about. I would only have a very short amount of time to seal my fate: Keep my job and change the company or get fired.

I hit each point I wanted to make with only the bare facts, figures and results contained in past company financials. I presented a summary table prepared by my CPA which showed the disparity between what company profits were made, what profits were taken by George and what profits were owed to minority owners and employees. "In order to survive, prosper and experience sustainable growth, the company needs more fiscal transparency and consensus among the shareholders for decisions that affect everybody," I said, and went on to describe how we could do that. Finally, I demanded that past profits owed to minority owners and employees be paid by the end of the first quarter following the annual meeting.

George sat forward in his chair, looked me in the eye and said, "You need to leave, because you are a problem employee. According to others in the company, you are difficult to work with. In fact you are nothing more than a field technician, and I never wanted you or anybody as a partner. If I had to do it all over again, I would never have had partners. We'll transition you out of the company over the next several months."

In about a half an hour I had exposed my soul, asked for what I knew was legally mine, laid out my plan for a better future for me and everybody in the company, heard a pack of lies, got fired and lost my job. Now I stood alone, with only myself to blame.

Now I stood alone, with
only myself to blame.

I just sat in my office for about an hour without moving or saying a word, replaying the whole thing over and over in my mind. I was finally at peace with it all, but the peace came with a tinge of numbness. Once the numbness faded, I thought, *What on earth am I going to do now? I can't believe he really just fired me! Deep down, I knew he'd fire me if I pushed him to follow through on the agreements.*

I told the truth, and I got canned. So what, now what? I came up with a plan to work for the company as an outside consultant. I worked out which projects I would stay involved in, my hourly rate and the length of this new arrangement. I called all my clients and let them know that I was leaving the company, but the company would still be there for them and I would be available if they needed me. I said that the company I had worked for was a good one, and the people working in it were exceptional. I thanked each one of them for working with me, gave them my contact information and did not call them back.

But all that only put off acting on my own dream. About two weeks after my meeting with George, I sat bolt upright in bed at two in the morning with a burning desire to cut all ties with my old firm. Very early that same morning, I packed up all my things in my office, made copies of all the files I wanted from my computer and wrote a one-page resignation letter to George and my other partners.

I realized that I had to make a complete, clean break from my past so I could create a new future for myself. Playing it safe by working as an outside consultant with my former company was a distraction I could not afford. I needed to put all my energy into my own company, and I needed to start immediately.

I wrote my resignation letter on November eleventh, and on November seventeenth, I started my own consulting company, Trinity Source Group, Inc. When I received my articles of incorporation from the California Secretary of State, I was so happy, energized and fired up: My idea was finally taking on a tangible, real shape. My concept was now legitimate, and I felt confident enough to proceed. During those intervening six days, I had worked nonstop, thinking, planning and acting to start my own company. I had hit rock bottom; I had nothing to lose, and everything to gain. The only way forward was to succeed with my own company. I put all my focus and energy into that one endeavor.

Once I fully committed myself to my goal and dream of starting my own business, and cut all ties with all other income streams, things started to take off. As soon as I had an idea of what I needed, that very thing showed up. I took a chance, and bid on a two-year contract with a Fortune 500 oil company. It took twenty-seven hours of straight work to meet the deadline.

More than that, I battled with all sorts of doubts and fears about the job. I almost gave up because I was afraid I'd be unable to do all the work included in the contract documents. I was afraid I would fail. But I faced down these fears the same way I faced down the fear of meeting with George. I knew it was right for me to submit the contract and I knew I'd figure out a way to get the work done.

By the end of November, I had won that contract and a second contract with another Fortune 500 firm. And by the end of the year, I had many contracts with former clients; I was more valuable to them than I had thought. I had nothing to start out with but an old Dell desktop computer in the bedroom I rented from my

*We can truly have anything we dream about
or want, if we're willing to pay the price.*

friends and an aged Volvo station wagon. I did not have trucks, tools, equipment, banking, insurance, employees, payroll service, an accountant, an office or any of the normal, essential parts of a business infrastructure I knew I needed.

I was afraid, because I had stepped way out of my comfort zone. I was used to working with partners. Now I alone would be responsible for the success or failure of my fledgling business. I had no one to collaborate with, confide in or bounce ideas around with. What I did have was ten years of hard, honest work done with integrity and a true desire to help other people. This proved to be very valuable indeed.

As the contracts started to roll in, I used the line of credit from the house I owned to get an office and start building the infrastructure of an operating environmental consulting company. Within a year, Trinity Source Group, Inc. did more than a half-million dollars in sales and had four employees, plus me. The first year of business was very profitable and things have been going strong for more than six years now.

I cannot describe in words the feelings of joy, happiness and pure satisfaction I felt after my first year in business for myself. All areas of my life were renewed during that first year. It was an amazing period of growth and transformation for me. I've remarried and have a fulfilling, rewarding and growing relationship with my amazing and beautiful wife Catherine Byrne.

The universe wants to give us what we really desire. The trick is, we must want it badly enough to give up everything else for it. We can truly have anything we dream about or want, if we're willing to pay the price. There will be tests, trials and tribulations on the road to fulfilling our goals and dreams. These so-called tests are not obstacles put in our way to stop us from realizing our dreams; they're simply doorways we need to pass through in order to achieve them.

Dreaming, in and of itself, can accomplish nothing. We must first think to discover our dream; we must grasp it with burning desire. And then we must act to make that dream a reality.

Tap into what you really want, and develop a burning desire for it. Make a plan, take action and your vision will be realized if you're willing to pay the price, if you're willing to risk it all, if you're willing to step through the doorways.

David Reinsma is President and principal geologist at Trinity Source Group, Inc., an environmental consulting firm headquartered in Santa Cruz, California. He earned his BS in geology at California State University, Chico. In his twenty-two years in the fields of environmental geology and hydrogeology, David's work has focused on soil and groundwater assessment and remediation. David also works with Lifemax, as a distributor of the amazing whole raw food Mila, which has the highest plant-based Omega 3 content available. Connect with David at www.TrinitySourceGroup.com and at www.Lifemax.net/DavidReinsma/.

Kathy Quinlan-Perez

○ ⭐ ○

CREATING YOUR LEGACY

Legacies don't happen over night. A legacy is an idea that turns into a picture in your mind, that then becomes a driving passion of your intention, which, eventually, after you've taken consistent steps and held fast to your vision and inspired others to take up the charge, will become a legacy. Your dream becomes a legacy when it lives on in others.

"We've done this before. I know we can do this," I said to the eight San Francisco Police Department officers, sitting in their meeting room and looking at me with disbelief in their eyes.

"Who is this white chick from Hillsboro and what's she going to do with our kids from the projects?" their expressions seemed to ask.

Despite their good-humored doubts, these were the officers behind Operation Dream, a community outreach program I had been reading an article about only the previous week. Operation Dream was the reason I was even having this meeting; the SFPD Housing Authority police had started it in a bid to show the kids from twenty-one different housing projects around San Francisco that there was so much more to life than their pavement.

As soon as I really got to talking with these officers, good men who took kids from the projects on field trips to baseball games, fishing, and skiing, these officers who had inspired me to create something that could change the thought processes of these kids and, we hoped, change their very culture, I saw that they were guys who wanted to build a different relationship with their community. As soon as the kids saw them, they went running. The SFPD wanted to create a different experience of the police, to communicate that they were there to help, not to arrest. Once I explained my concept to them, the intention was set. Camp Choice was born.

In February I started making phone calls and by June some of the greatest minds in the country had been working with me to create an agenda and raise the funding for the camp. The officers

The first day was hellacious.

had been working to get the kids together; on the first day of the camp, the bus pulled up at PSI World Seminars' High Valley Ranch in Clearlake Oaks, California. We were ready—or so we thought.

The first day was hellacious. One of the volunteer camp counselors went to hug one of the first girls off the bus, and was told, "Get your f***ing white hands off me, b****." The rest of us stood there in shock; this was not looking like anything we'd ever seen before. By two o'clock that afternoon, when these kids had been running circles around us for hours already, the entire agenda was torn up. Clearly, one-hundred-percent intention had been set; however we had to be to get through to the kids, we would. He or she who is most certain wins.

That evening, when the kids were getting ready for bed under the supervision of the SFPD officers who had lent their time to the cause, we held a staff meeting in the ranch barn. I was standing outside trying to figure out what inspirational thing I was going to say that would get people motivated and excited to be here. When I walked inside, everybody looked like hell. In the end, it was my husband Gary who summed it up perfectly: "This is a football game, and we're in the first quarter. They are kicking our ass, and they are ten years old. So come on, people, let's get back in the game."

And somehow, through the different lectures, seminars and exercises we held, we got back in the game. Gary became the chief disciplinarian; though we punished bad behavior with timeouts and the like, we found a way to get through, to communicate to these kids that no matter how many timeouts they were given, they were not getting sent home because of bad behavior. They were not leaving and we were not giving up on them. Even Jovan, a kid who got timeouts every single day, learned this.

On the last day, we circled up and made a time capsule. We asked the kids to write down something that they wanted the world to know about them. We would seal the messages in a time capsule for the future. One of the messages read: "Good luck in your world. In my world, it's hell. Drugs, coke and crack-heads, that's my world. Everybody is killing each other, and it is hell. It's a shame, and I wish it could be better. Whoever finds this, take care of your world. I hope that I come back and read this as another person."

Before it was time for the kids to leave, I found five of the boys sitting on a tree stump in tears. This was probably the first time in these kids' lives that they felt safe and valued and that they mattered. At the ranch, they got three square meals. They didn't

"We want better for ourselves, but they won't give us a chance."

have to worry about hearing gunshots or someone coming at them. This was their ranch and they didn't want to leave. I promised them that Gary and I would take the five of them out to a movie.

When we showed up two weeks later, ten kids were there, including Jovan and his brother Johnny. After that, my husband and I took Jovan and Johnny under our wing. They were two struggling boys who desperately needed an advocate, someone they could turn to whom they knew would be there no matter what. But for all that we tried to teach them, particularly in light of their own teachers "forgetting" to put their grades on their report cards, they also taught us the absolute value of commitment to a cause.

When Johnny was arrested and sent to Log Cabin Ranch, an offset of the main juvenile detention facility, it led Gary and I to create another branch of our program. Families were allowed to visit on Sundays, but when I arrived to visit Johnny, because I wasn't an immediate relative, I wasn't allowed in to see him (and by this point, his mom had told me that if anything were to happen to her, she wanted me to be his legal guardian). Instead, they arranged for me to have access on Tuesdays, as his "counselor." Through these visits, I also got to know a lot of the kids there and designed and developed a Log Cabin Ranch program.

We took seventeen of the boys who were about to be released to High Valley Ranch, and some truly amazing and awe-inspiring things happened. One event we held involved using teamwork to get up and over a wall, in order to teach the importance of overcoming internal walls and the "three Rs" that were so prevalent in the projects' culture: resentment, resistance and revenge. Looking at this wall with the naked eye, anyone would balk. Yet two boys from the facility, one of whom had a relative who had killed a relative of the other boy, did it. I watched them pulling each other up and over the wall and was staggered at their sense of brotherhood and camaraderie.

One of the boys who attended that particular camp said something that has both stayed with me and continued to shape the intentions behind Camp Choice: "Out in the world, people look at us like we're animals, maybe because we're black or wear our pants too low. But the truth is that we want good lives, and families. We want better for ourselves, but they won't give us a chance."

There have always been challenges, of course, and I'm sad to say that I've been to my share of funerals. But we've also had our share of success stories, just from giving these kids a chance and showing them that "better" is within their reach.

One particular success story that's close to my heart is that of Jovan, whose high-school graduation I attended. Jovan had had his ups and downs, but had transferred to one of the top high schools in San Francisco and Gary and I saw him walk to get his high-school diploma. No one in Jovan's family came to see him graduate, but the sadness I felt for him was tempered when I realized, as we were driving him to see his sister so that he could show her his diploma, that we had still succeeded. Through what we had done, even though we might not be blood family, we were still family, and Jovan knew that.

Over the years, Camp Choice has evolved to be something beyond what any of us originally dreamed. This has taught me that, while to think is to create, once we create the picture, there is always room for evolution. The passion that my team and I have is creating a legacy—we have been there to make a ground-level

Creating a legacy is not a goal; it's a life.

difference in the world, and I believe that is what anyone with a dream does in achieving it. When I'm personally invested and emotionally connected, there is nothing I can't do. Creating a legacy is not a goal; it's a life. The legacy of Camp Choice is that it will live on without me, that it will live on in the children who have made our vision their own.

Jovan's success has opened my eyes to the success of the program as a whole. At the 2012 camp, when Carson Johns (one of the first graduates who fully supported the program when we were just getting started) was making introductions, he said, "It's a monumental year for us because one of the first girls who came to the ranch... Well, her son is here, and another girl, her daughter is here."

Holy Toledo, I thought. *They're seeing such values here that they're making sure their kids go.*

The saying is true: It takes a village to raise a child. They're the ones creating the future. They have taught me about patience and compassion and about not letting a dream get away from me just because I might encounter obstacles. Having a dream and making it happen is like learning to walk: You wouldn't give up on a child taking those first few steps, so why would you give up on your own dream? Over the last eighteen years, I've learned that my passion to leave a legacy is my fuel. Could it be yours, too?

Kathy Quinlan-Perez is a PSI World Seminars instructor and the co-founder of Camp Choice, a yearly project for underprivileged youth, which has been running for eighteen years thanks to the generous donations of PSI World Seminars graduates. For more information and to connect with Kathy, go to www.CampChoice. org.

Operine Banton

───── ○ ✦ ○ ─────

TO WALK WITH ANGELS

I learned very early in my life that the old adage is true—life is a journey, not a guided tour. The earliest example of this that I can remember is from when I was six years old: My parents moved to England from our native Jamaica, leaving my five siblings and me behind. I recall watching my mother leave, thinking that she was just going to the village market. When she did not return, I wondered if I was not really her child either—as my father had told me countless times by then, I was not his.

At age twelve, when the weary caretakers with whom I was left had finally grown tired of the way I drifted, I was sent to join my parents— one of the last of my siblings to do so. Upon moving to England, I felt both lighter and heavier at once: Relief at a respite from the many forms of abuse I had suffered while in Jamaica was tempered with the familiar ache of being adrift. I never had a vision for what I wanted to do with my life. It was my English teacher— one of many whom I now refer to as my angels and guides—who thought I would make a good nurse, but then again, that was all that was available to a black woman in 1960s England.

When I made my decision, I was left with my father, who was supposed to take me to the nursing school while my mother and siblings left for Jamaica for the holidays. He started leaving me alone in the house to go out with his drinking buddy. Two days before we were to leave for school, he came home drunk, ranting and raving that he had promised me to someone and I had gone against him. (Years later, I learned that he had promised me to his sixty-five-year-old drinking buddy. He thought I had gone off and got myself pregnant, which would have cost him his free alcohol.) The next thing I knew, he was holding me by the neck and choking me until I passed out.

I came around two days later, on December twenty-ninth, with an overwhelming sense that I needed to leave. I managed to get

The next thing I knew, he was holding me by the neck and choking me until I passed out.

myself to the nursing school, where the doctors and nurses took care of me for two weeks until I was fit to begin my training. I didn't return home for two years, and it was only when my mother called the hospital looking for a grandchild that I learned my father had told her I was in a home for unwed mothers in North London—I returned home briefly to set the record straight.

After I qualified as a nurse, I still spent many years emotionally at sea due to the long-lasting effects of the problems I had with my father as a child. Hearing him say that I was not his child so often, and for so long, left me feeling totally unlovable. *Nobody wants me; nobody cares for me,* I thought. I couldn't connect with anything—I believed I didn't belong anywhere, to anyone. I moved around a lot, unable to trust or form real, solid relationships. In my life, I married twice and had three children; yet still there was a major part of me that never trusted in the connections I formed.

Slowly, over the course of the many years I spent drifting, my relationship with my mother reached a plateau where she became the glue that held me together. She kept me going. Somehow, even when I was living in Canada with my first husband, she knew all the way from England if I was unhappy. She could always tell when she needed to contact me—I'd be sitting at home worrying about something, and the phone would ring.

In 1985, when she passed away, I was completely lost. It was as if there was nothing to hold on to. My sister was the one who called with the news, and I immediately went home to grieve with my family. After the funeral, my father and I were sitting outside on the veranda, and we shared a moment that changed my whole life. "You are the only one of your siblings that is like your mother," he told me. "You are forgiving, and loving, and you care about people just like her."

In that single moment, he went from staunchly denying that I was even his child to honoring me for being like my mother; it was in that moment that I realized: *I have forgiven him.* To hear those words from him felt as though he had given me a gift—I suddenly felt that I belonged to someone, and that he was suffering, too. This time, I was floating into a loving light for the right reasons. A terrible weight was—all at once—lifted from my shoulders. I experienced freedom at my core.

Things began changing very quickly after that, both within my life and within myself. Being given this gift of knowledge that I truly did belong to someone helped me see that I didn't have to stay a victim.

I started believing in myself, in my potential, in what I could do and achieve in my life. For the first time, I shook off my old, habitual doubts and became a woman with positive hopes and dreams for my future. I let go.

The first—and biggest—change that happened was my decision to go back to university. One cold day, I was walking with my children when we came across a woman standing on a street corner. Hung on a string around her neck was a tin can, upon which was written "Women's Shelter." I dug deep into my bag and gave her all the money I could find. A few days later, while working with two of my patients, they shared their experiences of sexual abuse with me.

These two seemingly unrelated events propelled me forward with a new sense of purpose—I was unsatisfied with nursing, and knew that I had something more to give to the world. The decision wasn't a difficult one: Everything at that point came together to tell me, "This is what you want to do, so do it." While continuing to nurse, I enrolled at university to study psychology.

During this time all of the memories of my own personal abuse—the memories I had worked for years to bury in a box deep in the back of my mind—came rushing back, and I was knocked sideways. Thankfully, I recognized that the only way I could go about dealing with and letting go of the trauma was to seek help from the counseling department. The counselor with whom I met—and to whom I owe a huge debt of gratitude—helped me more than I can say, and went on to aid my efforts in becoming a counselor myself.

*Angels come in many forms; they
do not have to be pretty.*

Shortly before I was to complete my master's degree, I found myself wandering off campus and into an area of the city which, I had been warned by many, was dangerous. Something—like a voice inside me—told me to go there anyway. Loaded down with my backpack, I walked until I came across a group of street men. Despite their haggard and dirty appearance, they all had kind eyes, and asked me what I was doing. When I told them I was attending university close by, they sent up a cheer and implored me to "Do it for us, sister. Do it for us all."

"I will," I promised.

Angels come in many forms; they do not have to be pretty. When I graduated, I started working at an agency that provided counseling services for children. There I met Sandy, who introduced me to PSI World Seminars. I cannot stress enough the importance of programs such as these—because of PSI, I was able to release the final invisible strings of shame, fear and guilt that held me back. It finally became clear to me who I am, and how to love that person. I became more attuned to both my body and mind, learning when to hold on and when to let go or find another solution. It was the most important step I took in becoming the person I am today—it helped me to let go, to trust and to forgive.

The day I left the agency to start my own private practice was one of the happiest of my life. All of the abuse I had suffered, all of the trauma I had worked through, all of the lessons I had learned about the journey we are all a part of led me to the path I was always destined to follow—the path that the angels and guardians in my life had been helping me toward. It was not easy; I came across obstacles, difficulties, potholes, mountains and valleys. But in sticking to my dream and my vision, I reached a place where I was able to dedicate my life to the service of others.

If my father and I had not had the tempestuous relationship we did, I would not be who I am today. Because of what my father did to me, I arrived at a place of wanting to help people. Life, for me, is about service, and I don't think I would have learned so much about service if I didn't have those interactions with my

*Letting go of your past is not
simply forgetting about it.*

father. Now, when clients come into my office and say, "I feel like nobody loves me," I can empathize with them—relate to them on a different level.

Letting go of your past is not simply forgetting about it. Letting go of your past means scrutinizing it, learning from it and accepting it as part of yourself. Letting go of your past means releasing the pain and heartache that you have experienced, acknowledging the obstacles and fears you have overcome, and ultimately taking what you have learned and using it in your life to further yourself and, in turn, to help and serve others. When you start on this journey, know it is not a linear path. It is cyclical: you let go, and you serve, and in serving you are able to let go more.

Life may not be a guided tour, but when we let go of our past, we reap the benefits of our complete journey. All of our angels, "pretty" or not, are part of a well-planned journey, and their influence remains. Recently, I found myself lost en route to a retreat on one of the many islands near Vancouver, British Columbia. In the dark and rain, I stopped at a house to ask for directions, only to be chased off by a dog. As I drove away terrified, tears streaming down my face, various smells wafted in through the windows: the smells of fish, cigarettes, alcohol and flowers. I turned off the noise of my fears and tuned into the present. I relaxed, and let my mom and dad lead the way. You see, my mother smoked and made beautiful flower gardens, and my father was an alcoholic and loved fishing. I laughed all the way to the retreat. Secure in my warm cabin, I thanked all of my angels for guiding me home.

Operine Banton owns her own private counseling practice and is President of the Tri-City Business By Referral Association, a nonprofit organization that exists to help people build businesses. Connect with Operine at www.MandalaCounselling.com.

Randy Djernes

○ ★ ○

JUST LIKE ME

I was eleven that year. It was 1960, and we lived in a small town in Texas. Life had been good. Our house was the nicest one in Belton, with the only swimming pool in town. Dad had three successful Ford automobile dealerships in Bell County. Mom was president of the PTA at our school and a Girl Scout leader. Everyone in town knew us and our parents often had parties. Each year Dad gave Mom a new Cadillac. We traveled to Dallas to buy our school clothes in Dad's Cessna airplane.

My grandparents, aunts, uncles, cousins and family were all close. Every Sunday we all had dinner at my father's parents' cotton farm. Each of my grandparents' three sons, with their wives and children, would drive out to the farm and spend the day together. My brother Mark and I always looked forward to Sundays with Maama and Papaw.

I believed I was the most intelligent, creative child in the world. Everyone loved me, and everything was the way it should be.

I was the first grandchild and, after raising three boys, both grandparents doted on me. Many of my days had been spent at the farm with them while my parents attended social events. We made rag dolls in the shade of the porch. I rode on the back of the tractor while Papaw plowed, or Maama and I picked peaches from the orchard and vegetables from the garden. Papaw might take me to the store in his 1939 pickup and let me pick out a bag of two-for-a-penny candy. Sometimes we just sat around while Papaw told stories, or Maama sang to me the songs of her childhood. There was no television or indoor plumbing; water was hauled to the farm weekly and the radio didn't work consistently. But I always loved my days with my grandparents.

On the day everything changed, bluebonnets covered the roadsides and fields. It was hot and my parents were arguing again. When we arrived at the farm, Maama was still working the butter churn, getting the food ready for supper.

Papaw had come in from plowing, dressed in his overalls, tan and smiling. He gave me a hug and surprised me by saying, "We have a huge watermelon for dessert."

When my younger brother Mark went to bed that night, I sat in my bedroom enjoying playing with my dolls with my window open so I could smell the gardenia bush outside. The arguing got louder. I heard things breaking. I ran into the kitchen. Mom and Dad were

Life had changed suddenly and dramatically.

screaming. Mom was trying to kill Dad. He was chasing her with a knife. She had hit him on the head with the coffee pot and he was bleeding all over the floor. Running and standing between them and begging them to stop didn't help; it never had. After a while Dad took off in his car and Mom came into my room. "Your dad and I are getting a divorce. You and Mark and I are leaving soon to live in Oakland, California. That's where I grew up."

I did not know what a divorce was; no one I knew had divorced parents. But if the violence stopped, I figured that it might be a good thing.

Mark refused to get on the Greyhound bus. Mom pulled and pushed and he finally gave in. It was a long two-day trip to California, with lots of stops and no money for food. Exhausted, we arrived in Oakland and my mother's sister picked us up. The next day she took us to our new home, a small apartment up three flights of stairs in the middle of the city. Mom started her job working in her sister's jewelry store; we were registered in a new school. Life had changed suddenly and dramatically. Mom had always liked to drink, but now the drinking got out of hand and often she didn't come home from work. Mark and I had each other. We found lots of ways to get by. If we walked to school, we could save the bus fare and stop at the bakery to get a nickel's worth of day-old goods, our favorite breakfast. Soon Mark got a paper route; I babysat.

That first year Dad sold all his businesses in Texas. He remarried and moved to Tampa, Florida, where he bought a small airport on Davis Island and opened an aircraft dealership. He

My path to claiming my
power was not simple.

began racing a Ferrari, transporting it from track to track in his custom DC4 airplane. His pilot experience in WorldWar II led him to transporting cargo worldwide—and some of that cargo was unsavory.

My dad and I are both tall; we look a lot alike and have the same personality. He was an intelligent, multi-talented, charismatic man who could sell ice to Eskimos. But he was a complicated person who led an adventurous, dangerous life filled with money, marriages, girlfriends—and some very bad choices. My brother and I saw him at Christmases, but he was consumed by his new life and family.

Mark was Mom's favorite. He was tall and good looking, resembling her father. I looked more like my father's side of the family. It wasn't long before Mom began to transfer her anger toward Dad to me. Every day, angry and drunk, she would scream, "You're just like your dad…"

I couldn't stop her, so I began to try harder, avoiding any confrontation, attempting not to make any mistakes that would awaken her wrath and encourage her to blame me for her situation. She had not found "Mr. Rich and Right," but was busy searching the bars for him. I wondered: *I am* like Dad; will I make bad choices, too?

The night Mom pushed me through the plate-glass window in the motel, I was seventeen. It was midnight. She came in from the bar angry and awakened me by screaming and pulling my hair. "Your father is a no-good son of a bitch and you're just like him."

I tried to get to the office phone to call for help.

She chased me, yelling, "You're no good. You've given me nothing but trouble, just like your father."

I ran out the door in my pajamas and, down the dark streets filled with prostitutes and drug dealers, ran the whole six terrifying miles to my aunt and uncle's house, where they let me sleep through the night. And in my mind the echoes rang, "Just like your father; nothing but trouble..."

The next day my high school boyfriend helped me rent a studio apartment in a nice neighborhood. A few weeks later, skipping the all-night graduation party, we drove to Mexico and got married.

Forgive, forgive, forgive—but sometimes remember.

He came from a good family, had been my only boyfriend and was leaving for San Jose and college. I was not in love; he was my exit plan.

The next seven years were filled with college, work, marriage, financial struggle and the birth of my son, Scott. I believed that my children came first and that it was most important to treasure your family and make your home a sanctuary. At age twenty one, I founded the Young Mothers Association. The association grew to two hundred moms and I was president of it for three years. Our mission was to help mothers and children, support the growth of Montessori preschools and create responsible daycare for working mothers while providing a support group for other young mothers.

Mom was still angry, a friendless victim, single and looking. We still had a relationship—I was all she had—but I never again had the loving mother I knew in Texas. Her self-medication, lack of compassion and mental turmoil had progressed to a loss of contact with reality. I now struggled daily not to become the person she constantly accused me of being, the disaster she created in her expectation that at any time I would prove to be someone dangerous, evil and "just like your father, a no good son of a bitch." A child remembers a positive comment, but never forgets a negative one.

After seven years of struggle in a loveless marriage, at age twenty-four I had grown stronger and found the strength to start over with my young son. A month after my divorce became final, I met my husband, Bill. That night was the beginning of a lifelong

---

What we believe ourselves to
be is what we become.

---

love. During almost forty years with Bill, raising my son Scott and our three children, I have found my power as a woman, wife, mother, compassionate friend, successful businesswoman and community leader.

My path to claiming my power was not simple. It took years. For thirty years I volunteered in the public school system, attempting to prove to myself that I was a good person by improving public education. And I learned: Everything is negotiable but has a price; any task starts with a first step towards completion; diligence is often more valuable than experience.

I suffered five miscarriages, debilitating illnesses, multiple surgeries, heartbreaks, the deaths of family and loved ones and financial challenges. And I learned: Our trials teach us, often more than our triumphs do; marriage lasts when both partners find the needs of the other more important than their own.

For a lifetime, I struggled with poor self-esteem and accepted guilt. My relationship with my mother never improved, but continued to spiral until she was diagnosed as paranoid schizophrenic, bipolar and a danger to herself and others. Only after her official diagnosis and confinement to a mental institution could I accept that I would never, in her mind, be "good enough;" that it was she, not I, who had created her reality. And I learned: When you see yourself as a victim, you avoid accountability; forgive, forgive, forgive—but sometimes remember; you must define yourself and what you stand for, and not leave it up to others.

I had accomplished great things in my life and won prestigious awards, but I still heard the echoes: *You're just like your dad. You can't do that; you'll get it wrong, just like your dad. You'll make a disastrous choice, just like your dad.* Then I joined PSI World Seminars and saw Jane Willhite and Shirley Hunt and other strong women—capable, powerful executives.

Jane would tell me, "Please do this."

And I'd hear those echoes and be terrified that I'd get it wrong, fail, be fired. "Jane, I can't do that; I've never done anything like that before."

Jane would reply, "Sure you can. I have confidence in you."

I so admired Jane that I always tried. Maybe I could do some part of what she wanted. So I'd take the first step. And then, diligently, I took the next, and the next.

Each success softened the echoes. I saw how what we believe ourselves to be is what we become. I now believe in myself. I can do what I want to do and still have everything I want—I can care for my family, play with my grandchildren, cook dinner and still be a success at my profession. I can make choices that are not only good for me, but for other people. I believe that I am kind, warm, loving, humble, unselfish. I am a person who keeps my word and am a good friend. I enjoy caring for people and have few material needs. I'm fine with me. I'm especially proud of how I've raised with my kids, who are wonderful.

And I am like my dad, too—I'm brilliant, charismatic, adventuresome and good-looking!

I've moved Mom to a care facility just seven blocks from my house. She would greet my daily visit with a laundry list of complaints.

I'd say, "Mom, we all wake up on the same planet. I'm going to make my day pleasant. Why don't you do something you like, maybe a craft or some gardening?"

Any change takes diligence, but it does pay off. On my most recent daily visit, I brought Mom a scarf and a goodie bag of cosmetic items. For the first time, she sat with a group of other ladies in wheelchairs. I suggested that she share some of her goodies, and she did. I put on her new scarf and the nurses admired it. I kissed her cheek and turned to go.

She said, "Don't forget me."

You are not "just like" anyone. Believe in yourself. Follow your passion with diligence.

Randy Djernes has been a child advocate and mentor for children at risk for twenty-five years. She is an activist for education funding in California and a pro bono grant writer for community nonprofits. Founder of the Cupertino Young Mothers Association and the Lake County Foundation, she is a three-time nominee for "Woman of the Year" Stars of Lake County, was awarded the International Peace Award from Naka-cho Prefecture in Japan, and was given an award by the U.S. Senate for community service and lifetime achievement. Randy manages High Valley Ranch and is a former member of the governing board of Middletown School District and a former northern California representative on the California School Board Association. She has also served on the Democratic Party Central Committee. She is married to Bill Djernes and has four children. Connect with Randy at www. PSIWorldSeminars.com.

Josephine Johnson

SEE THE HAY IN
THE BARN

When I attended a PSI World Seminar in February of 1978, my life changed forever. My world opened up to infinite new and exciting possibilities: I now knew how to believe in me.

Using affirmations, I found the courage to say what I needed and share my feelings freely and honestly. All my relationships began to change for the better: my relationship with myself as a woman; with my loving, supportive husband of seventeen years, Frank; with our three beautiful daughters and with the rest of our family and friends. As I felt myself flooded with thankfulness for all that I had in my life and all I wanted to give to others, my prayers and connection with God became important again. I was growing, on the move.

I wanted Frank to share all this with me, so I asked him to go to the seminar. He did, but at the end of the first night, he hurried to our '62 Pontiac, unhappy because it was late, the drive home would take an hour, and he had to be at work in just two hours. "I'll finish this, but I'm going to get my money back," he said.

Disappointed, I hung my head.

"Look up," Frank said. "Talk to me."

Wow, this is different! I thought. *Things are already changing between us.*

We talked the whole way home.

By the end of the first seminar, Frank loved and valued PSI so much he declared that our three daughters, then aged sixteen, fifteen and thirteen, would all go the following month. Then, Frank and I attended PSI 5, PSI 7 and Founders (PLD) together. It was like falling in love all over again. The kids went to Teen Camp with Frank as a staffer, and I went to the Women's Leadership Seminar. Eight of my sisters and brothers, my mom and dad, Frank's sister and her children and lots of friends went to PSI 4. So many lives were changed. This was the groundwork for the challenges to come.

Just a year later, in 1979, Frank and I attended a PSI Founders' ninety-day goal-setting class. During the class and later at home, we talked about buying our neighbors' home and feed store across

My world opened up to infinite new and exciting possibilities: I now knew how to believe in me.

the street. It had been for sale a while. Maybe we could work together one day, build something lasting. We visualized chatting with customers, strengthening community bonds and supporting neighbors.

One afternoon, I went across the street to ask Gloria how much she and Neal wanted for their property. "You guys don't have any money, do you?" she said, smiling.

"Well," I said, "We're in this class." I explained our vision. "If the price isn't prohibitive," I told her, "I know we could get a loan."

"I would love for you to have it," Gloria told me. "We just lowered the price yesterday, from two-hundred-twenty-thousand dollars to one-hundred-fifty-thousand."

When I went back across the street and told Frank the new price, he said, "Tell them we'll buy the place!"

Back across the street I went. "We'll take it!" I beamed at Gloria.

She yelled to Neal, "Tell that other buyer it is SOLD!"

I felt my stomach turn upside down with excitement. Our vision was already coming into being! Hooray!

Using the techniques we were learning in PSI, and with much support from our PSI team, we achieved our goal and purchased our two acres with the house and feed store. This was an incredible accomplishment, as we had only about twenty dollars in the bank at the time! But the bank approved the mortgage, provided we paid off our new car. We did that, and our cushion was gone, with only a hundred dollars left for inventory. We sold our boat. Frank had a great job, so we moved forward. Johnson Feed was born.

Neal said he would teach me the ropes for thirty days, things like what to stock and how to buy trailer loads of hay. What a blessing that was, since Frank continued working for Crane

Maybe we could work together one day, build something lasting.

Services as I ran the business. I loved it—chatting with my neighbors, caring for their animals, hiring the boys from the high schools and sharing PSI with everybody I talked to. It was so much fun—and very scary. After eighteen years as a stay-at-home mom and photographer, I was really doing it! I felt deeply thankful for PSI Women's Leadership and all those years my dad grew alfalfa out in Arizona. As I drove out at five in the morning to pick out the best hay from the brokers, I kept saying my "I AMs" and my affirmations, including: SEE THE HAY IN THE BARN.

Then I received a notice from San Bernardino County, saying that the feed store property was not zoned commercial. We could either pay a fine of a thousand dollars a day and keep the store open or close it immediately. I was shocked. We'd been buying hay from Gloria and Neal for years, just like everyone else! *What will we do?* And then: *There must be another way.* I knew after the PSI classes to go to my inner vision, where solutions were endless; my intention was one-hundred percent to have Johnson Feed. I called the county.

"Sue the people you bought it from," they advised.

"No way," I said. "They are our friends."

103

A man at the county told me that if I was in the process of getting a zone change, they couldn't fine or shut us down. But as I tried to change the zoning with the county, the city decided to fight us. I defended Johnson Feed with seven-hunded-fifty neighbors' signatures and the visionary persistence I'd learned from PSI. It took a total of five years for us to get the proper zoning approved by the city and the county, but we finally did it.

Then disaster struck again, and Johnson Feed was in trouble in a whole new way. After the long zoning battle, I had lost full focus. I was sixty-five thousand dollars in debt and couldn't pay my bills on time. Every lawyer we talked to advised us to declare bankruptcy, but that wasn't an option. *Now what?* I called Gail, a great friend who rode horses with me and who had trusted in me enough to start on her own journey with PSI.

Gail listened to my story and said, "Well, you have to eat crow."

"What does that mean?" I asked.

Gail said, "Go to everyone you owe money to; give them each an eighteen-month note on the feed store property. Pay cash for each load of hay—and stay focused."

I was so scared; I didn't want to eat crow! Then I remembered I had to get out of the worry and straight back into the goal. On my way to pick up grain, I started saying to God, "Thank you—thank you for that tree; thank you for the sky. Thank you, God, for everything." I laughed: *Wow, when did God get in there on the drive to pick up grain and eat crow?*

Taking Gail's wise suggestion, I went to all the hay brokers with an eighteen-month note on the property and the one-hundred-percent intention to pay them all back and make the situation a-win-win for all of us. Having to quit PSI facilitator training to focus on turning the business around broke my heart, but I also knew it was temporary. At the end of the eighteen months, I had paid back all the debt. On the very last day, after the banks closed at three, I took the last check for ten-thousand dollars to Quality Hay. John and Hank thanked me and said, "It is so nice for someone to keep their word. We have faith in people again." I was moved to tears.

I ran Johnson Feed for nine years, using the tools I received in PSI seminars. I learned to believe in myself and cross out the obstacles in life with a big sword in my mind and move on to success, seeing the perfect end result. Frank and I sold the business and the property for what would eventually amount to six-hundred-thousand dollars, and we're retired now. We have been married for fifty great years, and are surrounded by so much love. We also have liberty, a home, a rental, Frank's shop, an RV, a boat and various other vehicles, all paid off. We learned a lot from being in trouble financially!

I am Steamboat Josephine and I never give up, no matter how scared I am. If we hadn't learned and trusted the concept "to think is to create," my husband and I would not have ventured into a new, beloved business. We would not have shared PSI's life-changing effects with all those near and dear to us. I would not have believed in myself enough to love the at-risk teens I have been honored to

Be persistent, don't give in to
fear and never give up!

work with or to run for public office and win. My upbringing said women were important only in the home—but Jo Johnson became Josephine Johnson, proud to be a woman and a leader.

Persistence, focus and visualizing the hay in the barn and a happy end result have really worked to make my dreams come true. These tools can work for you, too, and I've seen them work for the thousands of people I've met through, and introduced to, PSI. Be persistent, don't give in to fear and never give up! That's what I tell the teens I work with, my children and my grandchildren, to help them go for their dreams.

Get excited about yourself! When you're excited about moving forward, and you can visualize your goal, you will persist even when problems come up. In other words, you'll think outside of the box. If you see one road ahead and then discover that road is closed, what else can you do? To think is to create—you can stop, look around at the wide world of possibility and move beyond that box.

Your single dream breaks open your life. You are worthy of being the person you want to be. Don't be scared to go for your dream; be strong and courageous. I challenge you right now to step into joy! Decide you want more, get a clear picture of your vision, take the PSI Basic training, move on to the advanced classes and go back and re-audit often. Go to that quiet place in your mind at least twice a day. Keep learning, giving, thanking, laughing, smiling and taking a step every day—no matter how small—toward your goal. Enjoy the journey of your life. Share your inner joy!

My purpose is to love God with my whole heart, soul, mind and strength and to love my neighbor as myself. Wow, that means I have to love myself! I do that by saying my affirmations, my "I AMs" and my prayers for each and every person in this world every day. So know you have been prayed for and wished well. I am excited for you—this is the best time to be alive. Hooray!

Josephine Johnson has been a devoted PSI student, volunteer, staff member, seminar leader, speaker and facilitator for over thirty years and has devoted much of that time to helping at-risk teens as a counselor and tutor in the Los Angeles area through programs like Options for Youth. An entrepreneur who built Johnson Feed from a vision into a more-than-half-million-dollar business, Josephine was the first woman to be elected to the Monte Vista Water Board and served as its director for fourteen years. She was also the first woman to serve on the Board of Chino Basin Watermaster, an organization formed to protect the largest groundwater aquifer in Southern California. She now travels with Frank, her husband of fifty-one years, and enjoys spending time with her children, seven grandchildren and many friends. Connect with Josephine at www.HayInTheBarn.com.

Gabriel DiCristofaro

○ ★ ○

LOVE OR FEAR?

G rowing up, I was a nomad and a keen observer and scholar of social dynamics. As you will learn from my story, it was literally a matter of survival for me.

I spent my life seeking—seeking to understand human relationships and interactions; seeking to use my talents, curiosity, energy and experience to make a difference in the world; seeking my purpose. I believed I was underperforming in life, until a major convergence of events changed everything: a difficult break-up followed by an injury (broken ankle) that forced me to stop everything and heal for three months.

During the healing, high up in my twelfth-floor apartment, I used the time alone to reflect on my life and failed relationships. I read books about body language, dating and relationships, all filled with useful information about mating customs and the social skills needed to find love. The more I read, the more things began to click: I quickly gained understanding of the causes of my past breakups and, more importantly, I began to write.

Lying on my blue couch, surrounded by books and manuals, I scribbled feverishly on countless yellow notepads. The words poured out of me. *What if I could help women attract the men of their dreams? What if I could help women invite real, lasting love into their lives?*

My ideas came out fully formed into a structured curriculum of classes and seminars aimed at showing twenty-first century women the power they have to attract good men in the modern world.

As I was creating the coursework, I struggled with doubt: *Why would any woman come to MY course to get matchmaking and dating insights?* The answer was clear: My years of experience and passionate observation allowed me to fully understand how men and women socially interact.

I saw that people act from one of two instincts: love or fear.

Growing up, the only consistent female role model I had was my mom. I was born in Chicago, Illinois, the only child of a single, nomadic woman. During my childhood, I was along for the ride as she hitchhiked around America, living in the poor neighborhoods of Indianapolis, Indiana and Boston, Massachusetts, where I often found myself the only white kid in a troubled black and brown community. In juxtaposition to living in what some would call the ghetto, my mom devoted most of her income to sending me to private schools with wealthy kids who appeared to come from stable environments and loving homes.

Because we moved around so much, I went to fourteen different schools before graduating from high school. In order to survive in my vastly different and hostile surroundings, I learned to read people's social signals.

I felt socially handicapped by my shyness and fear of rejection, yet I focused on watching and learning about people, especially first meetings.

I set challenges for myself by approaching and talking to strangers. As my confidence and understanding of social cues grew, I saw how much I enjoyed studying people's behavior and interactions. My biological need to have friendships and enjoy relationships drove me to overcome my fears.

My first major loss of love was with my mother. When I was eight years old, I came home from school one day to find my mother in the corner of her bedroom, hugging her knees and sobbing, with a large gun in her lap. She had tried to commit suicide with the machine gun she'd borrowed from a neighbor, a Vietnam vet, "for protection." The only reason she was still alive was because she hadn't been able to work the trigger safety.

I knew then that I was on my own because, at any moment, my mom could choose fear. She finally succeeded in taking her own life when I was twenty-three.

I had never seen my mother in a successful relationship with any of the men she dated during my formative years. Her fear of being alone made her seem desperate to me. Her values in choosing men were strongly distorted and ineffective. She had a couple of short-lived romances with good men. I was pleased to discover good men actually did exist, men who were polite, respectful, thoughtful and loving, and who even made me feel that way too.

To experience love, you have to understand yourself better, and if you're loving yourself, people will be attracted to you.

Unfortunately, they were just not matches for her and instead of discovering the reason why and attaining closure, she became frantic and depressed when these relationships didn't work out.

I saw that people act from one of two instincts: love or fear. For most of her life, my mother had operated from fear, and I spent a long time believing that I would follow in her footsteps. Thinking about what could have contributed to her loneliness and fear, I wondered: *Would my mother still be alive if she had known how to choose love?*

Most of us spend a good part of our lives denying that we are anything like our parents. The key difference for me was that I had learned at an early age to ask myself: *Am I acting out of fear or out of love?*

My mother had been an independent and progressive person, always standing behind women's rights and causes—causes which have also been close to my own heart. Through my mother's experience, I saw that the modern woman had shifted so much of her attention to the need for equality that she often overlooked learning about the dynamics of love.

As I wrote my curriculum, I saw how events in my life had given me the knowledge I now wanted to share with the world. Each life-changing event—moving often so that tentative friendships were left behind, dropping out of school as a sophomore to work and help pay the rent, being arrested for possession at nineteen years old—had taught me lessons about myself and helped me to realize the amazing person I was to become.

I moved from Boston to Los Angeles, California to escape the pain of my youth and the nasty weather that seemed to be a crippling force in my life. Los Angeles was a chance for sunshine, and I spent a few years as a working actor. Overall it was a good experience

Because I practice what I preach, I was able to attract the woman of my dreams.

and I grew leaps and bounds as a young man. I then settled in Colorado and finally left my inherited nomadic tendencies behind. The person I had become was someone who wanted to make a difference in the world, who knew just what kind of difference to make and, more important, was ready to do just that.

After taking a few select personal development courses, I found clarity on who I wanted to be and what I love doing. I became clear about my strengths and weaknesses. Both are equally important to understand about yourself. You must know yourself in order to be successful in any endeavor.

To change the patterns of the life you came from, you need to embrace the lows as lessons and the highs as wins. I learned how much I had to give, both as a person in everyday life and as a mentor to those around me. Considering everything I had learned from my mom's experiences and my own, I realized that I could help women understand the new social dynamics between the "modern woman" and the "modern man." I had spent years talking with strangers and fervently studying the social dynamics of men meeting women.

Making a difference, public speaking and helping women were the three key passions that drove me to create my future role, the role that would help me find my place in the world and allow me to help women with their love lives. Acting from the love I wanted to pay forward, rather than the fear and apprehension I felt, I told myself: *Nothing does it like doing it.* I began teaching the Inviting Mr. Right classes I had developed with all those yellow notepads, and was shocked at the level of positive response.

Once I hit my stride, I was fulfilling my purpose and living my dreams. Seeing people in love is one of my favorite things in the entire world. I love helping people be clear and find love. Every time women come to my class and gain a better understanding of themselves and men, I feel better. To experience love, you have to understand yourself better, and if you're loving yourself, people will be attracted to you.

I gain immeasurably from the work I do. Each time I make a difference in a woman's life, it helps me heal my own wounds and get past the sense of confusion I carried around for a long time. I wanted to be the man who could save my mom from the choice she made. After she died, I asked myself, *Was there anything I could have done to save her?* In the years since, and through self-discovery, I've realized she was—as we all are—solely responsible for her own happiness and choices.

I've helped women invite love into their lives and, because I practice what I preach, I was able to attract the woman of *my* dreams. The first time I saw Nicole, she was walking into a Halloween party in a 1920s zombie flapper costume with one of those dresses that has hundreds of tassels shaking on it. I immediately decided: *I'm going to meet her,* even though I was thinking it would probably be another of those two-minute conversations that never turn into a long-lasting relationship. It was a lively party, so I didn't see Nicole again until a couple of hours later. Without thinking, I blurted, "Where are you going?" as if it was obvious she had to stop right there and meet me!

We talked a little bit, and she asked, "What do you do?"

"I help women find better men," I told her, and she started laughing—in the best possible way.

We went on a few dates, and the checklist of things we had in common was staggering to both of us. We were an almost perfect fit. Every moment we were together, I was thinking: *Is this The Woman? Maybe I'll marry her.* I kept hearing myself ask her "the question," and one evening I accidentally referred to her as my wife to a group of buddies. I thought, *Whoa!* She wasn't my wife—I hadn't even asked.

The night I did ask her, I was excited because I had worked through my troubled conditions and conquered the fears and ignored the doubts, making it possible for my dreams to come true.

Fear or love? I chose love.

Would my mother still be alive if she had known how to choose love? I believe so.

Gabriel DiCristofaro is a social dating educator, life coach and the founder of Confidence UP. He has spent over twenty years researching, experiencing and training in his field. For more information on Gabriel's seminars and to connect with him, visit www.InvitingMrRight.com.

Alison Bechtel

A MATTER OF
THE HEART

I stared at the white stick, willing it to come up with the right answer, the answer that made sense. Instead I got the pastel wake-up call: two pink lines that told me my life would never be the same.

When the pregnancy test came out positive, my first thought was, *This is wrong. I have to go get a better test, because this thing is obviously not right.* I bought two more tests and my partner, Jon, watched with me as they both turned positive. *How could this be possible? There is NO way this is possible.*

As a kid, I always dreamed of being a really successful businessperson, and having an amazing family too. A Superwoman who could do it all and have it all: one minute creating a huge business deal, the next baking award-winning cookies; the next volunteering at a shelter with my kids and teaching them about giving back. But as I got older, that dream began to fade. As my business grew and my success came to fruition, my dreams of a family began to seem out of reach. I was constantly working to help others reach their goals, and I had put my own dreams on the back burner.

I longed for a relationship, a partnership in which we could both share our goals and dreams, that fulfilled me at home rather than just at the office; a relationship where we shared a vision—a vision that included raising a family. When I met Jon at a real estate convention, we hit it off almost instantly. It didn't matter that he lived a thousand miles away; I could literally feel the fireworks. It was the first time in my life when my almost-forgotten vision looked as though it could become reality.

Fast forward through months of long-distance dating, and I now found myself staring down at three positive pregnancy tests—but now that my childhood dream was an adult reality, I panicked. *What are people going to think?* I had achieved my vision

*I had put my own dreams
on the back burner.*

of becoming a successful businesswoman—I had a reputation to think about. *What are people going to think? How in the world am I going to do this? I am not married, and I'm always busy; what kind of life could I give to a child?*

As if three tests weren't enough, we went to Planned Parenthood for a fourth and final test, "just to be sure." That Friday afternoon, the waiting room was full of teenagers who looked at Jon and me with bewildered expressions, as if to say, "What are those old people doing here?" After another positive test, we were taken into a room with a counselor who talked me through my "options," and gave me tips on how to have a healthy pregnancy. She was surprised when I said, "I'm not sure I'm going to keep the baby."

Jon said, "I think it's great that you're pregnant, and it's something that could bring us closer together, but it's up to you." I was terrified and completely unprepared for a baby and becoming a mom. I made up stories in my head about what others would think. *How would the agents in my office, my colleagues, and potential agents perceive a knocked-up and unwed real estate broker? How would my family react?* Then I'd wonder about how they would react if they found out I had been pregnant and had an abortion. *How would I react, years later? Would I regret it?* I was nothing if not pragmatic, yet I still felt totally stuck.

The next day, I made the call to the clinic to ask about the abortion process. They said it was as easy as taking a pill. *Seriously?' No doctor visit? No D&C? Wow. It's too easy to end a life.* I did what I would normally do in tough or emotional situations: I went numb. Over the years, I had learned to distance myself entirely from anything emotional about a difficult situation and deal with it using only logic and rationality. I ignored my intuition to the point where closing off my heart became second nature.

My mind raced with thoughts to justify my decision. *This is better for all of us. This baby can't grow up with a father who lives in another state. I can't afford a child. How could I be a good mother and a successful businesswoman?* I called the clinic and told the woman on the other end of the line, "Okay. Let's do it today."

She paused for a moment before telling me they didn't do that procedure on Saturdays. I would have to wait until Monday.

I asked Jon to extend his stay, knowing that I would need someone to drive me home after the procedure. Faced with two more days of conflict, I tried not to agonize over the decision. I spent all day and most of the night going back and forth about my decision, playing the "what if" game. The longer I agonized, the more my thoughts kept returning to my nieces and nephews. How much I had loved them; from the moment they were born—I loved them like they were my own children.

This is something I've always wanted, and yet I'm denying my heart. Why am I doing this? I tossed and turned most of the night and, slowly, something inside me began to awaken. Something told me that Jon should catch his flight home and that everything was going to be okay.

Sunday morning after breakfast, I told Jon to book his flight and go home on Monday morning. "You don't need to wait for me, I'm not going to the doctor," I said.

He just looked at me, and asked, "Are you sure?" Three simple words, yet so loaded. I was about to make a decision that would alter the course of two lives, and bring a third into the world.

"Yes," I said. I had never been more sure of anything.

"Okay," he replied, and smiled. It was a beautiful moment between us; I realized that we didn't need a long, drawn-out conversation about what was logical or rational. We both knew we were going to keep the baby. This wasn't a matter of business; it was a matter of the heart.

We drove to Sedona for the day, and on the drive we had the opportunity to talk everything out. We both felt completely happy and content with our decision. We walked around Slide Rock, holding hands, just being together and loving each other. Jon took

*This is something I've always wanted,
and yet I'm denying my heart.*

some pictures of us, and my belly, and then we visited the Church in the Rocks and impulsively lit a candle for our family. "Wow," I found myself thinking. "Our *family.*"

Before that weekend, I had almost resigned myself to the fact that I would never have a family of my own. But as I watched that candle burn bright and strong for our future, I began to accept that I was pregnant. I was at peace, and very settled sharing that moment with Jon in which we got to truly connect and accept where we were going together. In that church, I began to feel again; throughout my pregnancy my inner voice only became stronger. I began weighing more decisions using my intuition as well as what I thought was practical. I started listening to the voice telling me that, even though I didn't know what was going to happen, I should go ahead and let it happen anyway—it was an awakening to my heart.

During my pregnancy, I learned to cry again. There were times when I would laugh one moment, and cry rivers the next. In the past, things like that would have really bothered me. But I could feel myself becoming more of a whole person throughout this emotional rollercoaster ride. I accepted it, and further, I became less judgmental of both myself and others. I realized that crying is okay—it happens for a reason, and it's a good thing.

Being able to access my emotions also changed my business life in a profound way. I found myself more readily able to connect with my colleagues, and I wasn't nearly as guarded as I used to be. I could communicate more deeply with my co-workers on a personal level, instead of on just a business level—something that I'd never been comfortable doing until I began listening to my heart.

Eight months later, I went into labor. I woke Jon at two a.m. to take me to the hospital. In the past, I hadn't been able to accept help, so the way he doted on me and was so loving and caring throughout the labor and delivery was a new and wonderful experience for me. He coached me the whole way through, and helped the nurses deliver our son.

After the birth, it was overwhelming to look at our beautiful little boy and know that everything could have turned out completely different. There was a moment when he was a few months old,

It was a new decision to listen to my heart, and it changed my life forever.

and I was sitting in a rocking chair and holding him, looking into his beautiful eyes. I said out loud, "Thank God I made the right decision." And I cried and cried and cried. It was a new decision to listen to my heart, and it changed my life forever.

Since then, Jon and I have had two more children together, all within three years –they are the loves of my life, my greatest blessings. Somewhere along the way I had decided to tune my heart out, and came to believe that listening to what others were saying (or what I thought they would say) was more important. But after trusting my heart and welcoming three children into my life, I now know that when you really start to trust yourself, it doesn't matter what other people think. I now know with certainty that I have all the answers I need. I don't need to look outside or to others for answers; I already know what is right for me. I just need to listen to my heart.

Listening to my inner voice has taken practice. The first time, that Sunday morning in Sedona, it was almost as if I could hear someone saying right into my ear, "You're not going to that clinic on Monday. Just believe in yourself." Since that very first decision, I've cultivated my inner voice and learned to trust it. Now, when something comes up and I'm nervous or fearful, I know that it's something that will move me forward. Those are the times of my greatest glory, the times when I'm totally scared to death and not quite sure what to do, if I should or shouldn't. That means I should. If I'm afraid of it, that means I have to do it. I trust my heart, and just do it.

I think often of that first pregnancy test and wonder what life would be like today if I hadn't listened to that voice. Where would I be? I wouldn't have my children around me, that's for sure. Could Jon and I have even stayed together after the inevitable wedge that would have been driven between us? I am so grateful that I had the courage, in that first moment, to not only hear that voice but also listen to it.

When the big, scary decisions have to be made, the best thing to do is let yourself be scared, listen to your heart and do it anyway. When you trust in your heart, a whole world of blessings will come into your life.

Sara — Let Your light Shine!

Alison Bechtel is an entrepreneur and consultant. Her passion lies in supporting business owners to use the power of leverage to create liberty, capture their dreams and live the lives they really want. Connect with Alison at www.AlisonBechtel.com and www.SupermomCEO.com.

Rhonda "Ronnie" Zaday

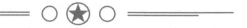

NEVER TOO LATE, NEVER TOO SOON

There it was. My name. On the ballot. Actually on the ballot. All the anxiety, the doubts, the fears, the just-plain-tiredness fell away in pure exultation. Without a huge bankroll, without "connections," I had gone where few women had gone before. My name was on the ballot in the race for County Commissioner!

I remembered my great uncle Leonard, who had been my hero and inspiration when I was a little girl. I had watched him as he chaired meetings of the bank's board, church committees and the directors of the county fair in our small Iowa town. I had been so proud of him when our brand-new fairground opened with space for more exhibits, a beautiful space for the community to come together and admire all of our varied talents! I wanted to be just like him. I wanted to wield that gavel and make a difference.

By the time I was a teenager, my dream had begun to fade. I had heard too often that I wasn't good enough, that "women don't do that."

In high school I led in many ways, but when it came to actually putting my name on a ballot, I jumped back and let others lead. My mom and stepdad nurtured my dreams, but my father and his family were always negative. My grandmother called me a stargazer, saying, "You're shooting for the stars, but you won't even make it to the moon."

After two failed marriages, I became the "trophy wife" of a successful executive who was nearly twenty years older than I. I had been successful in my work life as a salesperson, a mortgage broker and a trainer, but had never taken the next step to leadership. Now I was trapped in a beautiful house on top of a mountain in Pagosa Springs, Colorado. My husband expected me to do no more than keep house and maybe paint the picket fence while I waited for him to return from his business travels. I was depressed and demoralized, at the lowest ebb of my life.

But my dream of being a leader who would make a difference was not dead, only dormant deep in my heart. A friend dragged me to a PSI World Seminars Leadership Class. It was the best

I had heard too often that I wasn't good enough.

weekend of my life. I learned not to heed those who said I wasn't good enough. I saw that if I was being me, using the talents, the love, the passion and the determination I had been born with, I was so much more than enough for so many of the situations I had experienced.

Then I took a ninety-day PSI Leadership Development Course. Twenty or thirty of us took on goals and accomplished them with the help of buddies and coaches who challenged us on a day-to-day basis.

I started really using the visioning technique. I went to various community board meetings and visualized myself in the chairman's seat, holding the gavel, keeping a roomful of people on task, listening to all points of view.

I started losing the excuses; I banned words like "try" and "can't" and "but." My goal at the beginning of the course was to run for office in the metro district, or maybe even for the local water board. But, to my amazement, I was named the best team leader in the course and won several awards. I found people listened to my ideas and followed my guidance; I saw solutions to problems all around me—all because I had started loving myself unconditionally and allowing myself to be all I could be. I began talking with people in my community who could help me decide on my next step.

Usually, local politicians climb the steps of a ladder, serving on various boards and committees. I decided to leapfrog the boards and committees and run for Archuleta County Commissioner. Our county had few female board members, and had never had an all-female Board of Commissioners. In fact, there were only a handful of women politicians in the entire state.

Pagosa Springs is a small community in which many retirees have settled, and it caters mostly to vacationers. Inevitable growth was leading to turmoil.

Longtime residents wanted more and better jobs for themselves and their children. Retirees wanted to "close the gate behind them" and stop growth. Everybody wanted better roads and lower taxes.

Being a County Commissioner involves far more than attending a monthly meeting. It's a 24/7 job, with immense consequences. For instance, suppose there's a flood. It's up to the Commissioners to make decisions: to bring in the sandbags, authorize the

I started losing the excuses; I banned words like "try" and "can't" and "but."

sheriff's department and road crews, close roads, open emergency shelters and find the extra money to pay for all that's needed. The Commissioners' job is a daunting responsibility and an awesome challenge.

My mom and stepdad were completely supportive. Even my husband dove into the campaign. When I began, I didn't know how to run a campaign. All of a sudden, people just started appearing to help. They saw my confidence, my determination, my dream. A campaign organizer appeared; people started raising campaign funds and scheduling meetings. I was running against an incumbent who was one of the "good old boys." He was the strong favorite, because there was no place for a woman in small-town Colorado politics.

In a community that wants better roads, more jobs and more law enforcement—but no change—candidates are expected to take positions on critical decisions such as development, land use and zoning. I took a lot of hits. Dealing with other candidates and

We are so lucky to live in a country where everyone can speak up.

appearing on political forums was tough. Reporters scraped up every detail of my past and personal life, and that of my family. And over and over I heard, "A woman just can't win." I developed elephant-skin and held fast to my vision.

It had been a long, hard road, but now the campaign was over: In the quiet of the voting booth, I whispered a thank you to all who had helped make this moment possible—beginning with my great uncle so long ago—and pulled the lever next to my name.

When the first returns came in, I broke down in tears. I was losing! Was all that work, my precious revived dream, to come to nothing? I was a basket case. And then the tide turned. I edged closer, closer. Soon my numbers leapt higher, higher. I won by sixty-five percent!

The day I took the oath of office was one of the proudest and scariest days of my life. My mom, my stepdad and I, with my supporters and the other two women with whom I would serve in office, squeezed into the small courtroom. My stepdad stopped taking photos just long enough to say, "I've always believed you could do anything you set your mind to."

I served four tumultuous years as County Commissioner, on a three-woman board. I sat in that chair I had seen myself sitting in, listening to all opinions, making decisions. I guided the community out of the stalemate over development and changed some of the stagnant old ways things had been done.

Were my decisions always popular? No. Were they needed to correct many problems? Yes.

I found myself working with many different types of people, some who were there for their own agendas, and some who were there for the community. I found that even difficult people can have good ideas, and that people can be motivated to do the right thing when they see the right thing being done by people with determination. I found new opportunities to show others that they can achieve their goals, and that being a part of the solution, instead of just complaining, is the best way to change a challenging situation.

In today's political world, good people with their hearts in the right place are afraid to get involved, or even to take a stand, because of the attacks of the few and the unyielding press. But I took my

---

If you keep your dream in your heart, no matter how big or small, it's never to late and it's never too soon for it to come true.

---

stand. I did my job. I made decisions based on the information I had. As my former State Representative Mark Larson advised me, at the end of the day I could face myself in the mirror and know that I had done the best I could with the tools I had to make a difference for my community.

I continue to find opportunities to serve in the community. The choices I've made have allowed me to be where I am today, and open all the opportunities for me for great tomorrows.

So many of us sit on the sidelines. You don't have to become a senator or a president to make a real difference in your community. Begin going to meetings, and you'll see that speaking your opinion, sharing your thoughts, isn't so scary after all. If you're concerned about something at your local school, go to the school board meeting, listen to the issues and then speak up. If you don't like the way a road was paved (or not paved), go to the meeting and say so. That's how changes are made.

We are so lucky to live in a country where everyone can speak up. You have the freedom to be involved. Don't give that up by not using it.

Everybody has a dream; too many dreams lie crushed and dormant. But if you keep your dream in your heart, no matter how big or small, it's never to late and it's never too soon for it to come true. I think of the seventy-eight-year old woman who got her college degree, and of the ten-year old who helped save his grandmother's home from foreclosure. It's okay to be afraid. Be true to your heart. Once you believe in yourself, you can make a difference in many ways by just stepping up to the challenges.

Ronnie Zaday has lived in Pagosa Springs, Archuleta County, Colorado, for the past thirteen years. After working in sales and training positions around the country, she found a niche in the mortgage industry and progressed from the role of loan officer to owner of her own multi-million-dollar mortgage business, which she later sold to a major bank. Ronnie served as Archuleta County Commissioner for four years and is still active on several community boards. She is currently chairing the Southwest Colorado Workforce Board, and is Agency Manager of Wolf Creek Traders Inc., a freight agency for Landstar Trucking. Ronnie also recently opened a health and skin care business, with an emphasis on starting women in small businesses, and is writing a book about the impact women in local politics can have on the world. Connect with Ronnie at www.Zaday.com.

Matthew Chan

LIVE BY DESIGN

I could tell by the sound of her voice that something was wrong. In the two years since I moved to Toronto, my mother was always excited to talk to me and catch up on my life. This time, she seemed solemn. When I asked her if she was okay, she began to cry. She said, "I haven't heard from your father in almost a week."

My father was traveling in Thailand, following his lifelong dream to travel the world. He knew my mother would worry about him, so he was very conscious of the need to keep her up to date on how he was doing and his whereabouts, staying in touch with her regularly by e-mail. In his last e-mail, Dad had explained he was heading to Chiang Mai from Bangkok with some new friends.

I started to worry about Dad, but I kept thinking of rational explanations as to why he hadn't been in touch. *Maybe he wandered off to some rural part of Thailand and simply couldn't get to an Internet café to e-mail Mom? Maybe he's bedridden with food poisoning or illness.*

A week later, my brother, Elton, called me. "The Canadian Embassy says the Thai authorities found a body on the side of a deserted road," he said, going on to explain that the body was decomposed beyond recognition, and some of my father's possessions were found with it. The key item was his day-timer, which we knew he always carried with him. "They say whoever it is was robbed and murdered," Elton said, adding, "I just know it's Dad."

At first, I was stunned; the whole situation seemed very surreal. *This is the type of thing that happens to other people,* I thought. Then, anger bubbled up. *Why would someone kill my father? He was such a peaceful, friendly man.* Then, my feelings shifted to enormous grief. *I'll never see my father again.*

My parents emigrated from Hong Kong to Canada. My father, David Chan, was a man who relished simple pleasures. Music was

> *I will never, ever work for anyone ever again. Never again will I be at the mercy of someone else. I want to be the creator of my own destiny.*

his passion, especially from his favorite star, Elvis Presley. Dad had an amazing singing talent and was the hit at family gatherings or singing Elvis songs on karaoke night. He loved technology and was always interested in the latest thing.

My father's dream, though, was to eventually retire and travel. He fantasized about living in a Third World country, enjoying a simpler life. At an early age, I realized that my father didn't love, or even like, his work and was just counting down the days to his retirement. He was biding his time until he could finally follow his dreams and passions. It was because of this that I first wondered about working to live "someday." I thought, *Is this what I have to look forward to?*

Taking the advice I received from my parents—work hard, get a good education and find a career—I pursued a career in accounting after I completed my university degree and went on to earn a Chartered Accountant designation. After qualifying, I worked in industry for a couple of years and concluded that I wanted a different direction in my career. I just knew deep down I had a different calling for something more aligned with my strengths and interests. At the time, I just didn't know what it was.

In 2000, I took a big risk and moved to Toronto to work toward an MBA at the University of Toronto, Rotman School of Management. At the time, I was pursuing a career in finance. I was only a few months away from graduation when my father passed away, just five years into his retirement, five years of living his passions and dreams before his life was cut short. *I'll never get to see my father again,* I realized; it was a major wake-up call for me. I had just assumed I would have many more opportunities to see him—many more Christmases, many more moments after I graduated. Life is so fragile. Things can change in a moment; it's so easy to take people we treasure for granted. *There are so many things I still want to say to my father and do with my father, and now I never will.*

Still, I stayed on my chosen path and graduated with an MBA from Rotman. But, due to the many cutbacks in the economy and to other circumstances, my road after graduation was rocky. I

> *My vision of living by design meant that I would do something that mattered to me, something I was passionate about.*

eventually found a job, one I didn't enjoy, but still it was a job. When I was laid off just three months later, I was absolutely shocked and devastated. I hit a whole new low. When you are an MBA grad, you take pride in your career. It is what identifies you, and when you are not working, you feel empty and helpless.

Driving away from my now former office, I cried the whole way home. *What am I going to do with my life? Will I be able to pick myself up? Will I ever find a meaningful career and a purpose for my life?* I thought about my father; I didn't want to work for "someday" and wait until retirement to follow my heart. *I want to do it now.* In that moment I made a big decision: I will never, ever work for anyone ever again. Never again will I be at the mercy of someone else. I want to be the creator of my own destiny. I had no idea just how powerful and significant that decision would be.

Although I was very scared, I knew, deep down, that I had made the right decision. I knew if I didn't follow my heart, I wouldn't be able to bear the regret of wondering, "what if?" I didn't know what working for myself would look like or how I was going to get there, but I just knew it would happen.

At the time, my daughter Ashley was a newborn. I had a family to support, and I felt very lost and confused as to what to do next. After a lot of soul searching, I decided that I had to re-evaluate my future and ask myself some very difficult questions:

> *What is it that I want?*

> *What type of work would I enjoy and find gratifying?*

> *What am I good at?*

> *What kind of person do I want to become?*

This began my commitment to live a life by design, rather than by default. When you live a life by default, you react to the day-to-day happenings and the expectations that others place on you. A life by design, on the other hand, is a life of purpose and deliberate creation. Under this model, I live on my own terms and follow my heart; I don't let the expectations of others dictate how I live.

Living by design was a big step for me. With a professional accounting designation and an MBA, people expect you to have a certain career. My vision of living by design meant that I would do something that mattered to me, something I was passionate about. It would allow me to live the life I want now, not someday in the future when my work life was done.

I'm not living entirely by design as yet; these questions serve as a compass, giving me directions on how to plan and live my life. I wanted to own my own business with the opportunity to create unlimited income. I enjoy helping people and making a difference in their lives. Because of that, I'm good at solving people's problems.

Eventually, the Universe answered me and led me to a career as a mortgage broker, and I have not looked back since. I am very grateful to have found a career that allows me to engage, meet and support many amazing people. I have the freedom to structure and design my business the way I want. And being self-employed has allowed me to grow personally and spiritually, because it requires a lot of discipline and accountability to be successful.

These questions also help me stretch myself to activities that scare me, but that help me become the person I want to be. Because I wanted to become a better communicator, I confronted my fear

---

Once you make a decision that, no matter what, you will follow your heart, you'll be amazed by how easily everything starts coming together.

---

of public speaking head-on by joining Toastmasters and entering speech contests. Because I wanted to become a leader, I served a term on the Board of Directors for my industry's association. Because I wanted to become more fit, I have incorporated CrossFit into my life.

I still miss my father very much. Although it was a travesty to lose him, I am very grateful for the gift his untimely death has given me. There is nothing to wait for anymore. I am so much more aware of what it means to make life matter now, to live life with meaning and to confront my fears head on. Had it not been for this experience, I may not have cultivated the courage to take the risks I had to take in order to make a meaningful change in my life.

Ask yourself today what you truly want. What would you want to be different if you knew you couldn't fail? Once you discover that, make a decision that you will follow through and do something different. As I discovered, you don't need to know all the answers now or how it would have to look. It all starts with a decision— that is it. Once you make a decision that, no matter what, you will follow your heart, you'll be amazed by how easily everything starts coming together. That is how the Universe works.

Life is precious and unpredictable, and if you are waiting for a magic day when you can finally focus on what you really want, remember my father and realize, your "someday" may never come. Live a life of design, not a life of default. Start with your bucket list, your secret passion, your true north, your purpose, your calling, your deepest desires. And then ask yourself: "What am I waiting for?"

Dear Sara, live your life by design! Matthew Chan Principia 2012

Matthew Chan is a licensed sub-mortgage broker with Dominion Lending Centres, and a qualified Chartered Accountant (CA). He completed his undergraduate degree (BCom) at the University of British Columbia and holds an MBA from the Rotman School of Management at the University of Toronto. In 2011, Matt was recognized as one of the Top 75 Brokers in Canada by Canadian Mortgage Professional (CMP) Magazine. *Outside of work, Matthew is a family man, avid reader, Toastmaster, CrossFitter and poker player. His future projects include writing a book and creating a new blog. Matthew was raised in Vancouver, British Columbia, Canada and lives there now. To connect with Matthew, visit his blog at www.MattChan.ca.*

Curtis Takemoto-Gentile, MD

○ ✪ ○

EXPECT A MIRACLE

Everyday !

In 1991, on the Saturday afternoon of my PSI Basic Seminar, we were given an exercise: Come up with a goal, and start using the guiding PSI World Seminars principle—"to think is to create"—as the tool to reach that goal.

I was already successful and highly educated, in my dream job as an assistant professor in the University of Hawaii's School of Medicine. So I picked a lofty and "impossible" goal. *It would be the dream of all dreams to be promoted to the position of chairman of the University's brand-new Department of Family Medicine.* As a doctor, I was trained to approach everything with a healthy amount of skepticism. This awesome goal was a sure-fire way for me to prove "to think is to create" wouldn't work.

The requirements for the position filled half a page, and I possessed none of them. I hadn't even worked for the medical school for half a year, not to mention the fact that I didn't have the necessary training to create a curriculum for medical students or an accredited postgraduate residency program. I had no experience in hiring faculty, writing grants or starting a clinic, and I didn't feel confident about meeting the dean of the medical school, who would ultimately choose the qualified candidate.

What I did have was curiosity about this concept, "to think is to create." *Could it be possible? Could it be that easy?* Up to that point the only things I'd had time to read were medically related. I hadn't yet been exposed to Napoleon Hill, Og Mandino, Bob Proctor or any other teachers of prosperity consciousness. "To think is to create" just seemed too good to be true.

The week after I completed the seminar, my supervisor approached me in the clinic. "There's a luncheon to meet the dean of the medical school. Why don't you come with me and meet him?" I was stunned. *I was just thinking that the key to getting started was meeting the dean!* That was my first clue that "to think

---

*"To think is to create" just seemed
too good to be true.*

---

is to create" might actually get me somewhere. I did meet the dean—for about two minutes. In those two minutes, I found the courage to introduce myself and put forth my goal of meeting with him about the chairman's position.

I got what I needed: "Call my office to schedule an appointment." During that appointment, I shared my goal and my intention. I was honest, direct and enthusiastic and agreed with the dean that I didn't have the qualifications for the position. I also gave him all the reasons why I felt I did qualify and why I was the best candidate for the position. His final answer was that I had to be interviewed by the search committee and make their short list in order for him to consider me.

I wasn't deflated by this response. Instead, I was encouraged and extremely excited—after all, he didn't say no. This newfound attitude had only just been discovered—created—that Saturday at my seminar. I contacted the search committee, and despite all of my shortcomings, I made the short list!

At the end of my formal interview with the dean, he offered me the position on several conditions. "First, there are no funds to pay you a salary," he said. "Second, there are no funds to develop an academic department. Do you still want the job?"

"Yes," I told him.

Though I now understood why no one had filled the position for over a year, I was still very excited about the opportunity. After all, I was thinking outside the box!

"Finally," he said, "my expertise is in hematology and oncology. I will not be able to offer you any guidance in developing an accredited department of family practice." That meant I needed to develop both a curriculum for medical students and a post-graduate residency program on my own.

I was so excited! *Imagine: "to think is to create" got me to this part of my goal. How hard could it be to think and create my salary, funds to hire faculty and support staff and a clinical office? How hard could it be to think and create an academic curriculum and residency program that would meet all the accreditation standards?* I was experiencing a miracle, a dream come true; I would create a legacy for the state of Hawaii.

The creation of this department meant big things for the people of my home state of Hawaii. When I graduated from medical school in 1985, I wanted to be a family doctor. But at that time, Hawaii had no opportunity for family practice residency training.

I would create a legacy for the state of Hawaii.

Graduates like me, who were interested in family medicine, went away to mainland residency programs. Only a few of us returned because of the exponentially higher cost of living and forty-percent-lower salaries in Hawaii. Less than five percent of graduates went into family practice, because within the medical school we had no role models, no community and very few opportunities.

After I completed my family practice residency in Buffalo, New York my wife asked, "Where would you like to retire someday? Hawaii! Then why would we wait to live our dream until retirement?"

I saw her point, and I wanted to make a difference in Hawaii. Despite lucrative offers on the mainland, I decided to return.

My dream job at the time was actually to be in academic medicine. And I reached my dream; I became an assistant professor of medicine. I was broadly trained as a family physician in obstetrics, gynecology, pediatrics, internal medicine and geriatrics, and I even did home visits. Now I was teaching geriatric medicine as a family physician for the Department of Internal Medicine. Family medicine training is very different from internal medicine training; philosophically, we look at the whole family structure as a unit of care.

Creating the department from scratch was a huge challenge—the political and economic issues were monumental. To get something this big off the ground, I needed community support

*Intention is the most important
part of creating a dream.*

from internists, pediatricians, gynecologists, surgeons, hospital administrators and Hawaii's political leaders. Everyone needed to be part of an accredited department and residency training program. It was an incredible feat.

My new way of thinking always manifested what was needed in unexpected ways. I did create funding sources to cover not only my salary, but also salaries for the entire department faculty and staff, office space, several medical clinics and all the supplies and equipment. I accepted my opportunity with no financial support from the dean, the medical school, the University of Hawaii or the state legislature. And when I left, the Department of Family Practice annual budget was over eleven-million dollars.

One of the dramatic accomplishments of the newly accredited department was the increased percentage of graduates pursuing family practice as a career: It jumped from less than five percent to over forty percent. A second major accomplishment was graduating family physicians trained solely in Hawaii. A huge deficit in primary health care and education for the state of Hawaii had been filled.

I was ultimately unsuccessful in proving "to think is to create" was a fluke. Does it still work? In 2001, I started my solo medical practice, again with no funds. I left a government job, with all of its benefits—including retirement—for self-employment. After the success with the department, I knew it was time for me to pursue my life's purpose as a medical healer. I was told, "You're nuts." But I took the leap of faith and trusted again, wholeheartedly, in "to think is to create."

I have continued applying this simple principle in all areas of my life. Now it's hardwired. Initially, my challenge was in my doubts; what and how I was thinking was my failure, and now it is my success! It's what I teach my patients to overcome adversities. It's what I teach my children, and now I get to watch them create *their* dreams.

People constantly say to me, "You're the luckiest person!"

I always say, "It's nothing to do with luck. It's how I have trained myself to use my thoughts."

My question used to be, "What is the patient sick with?" which led to a diagnosis and a prescription. When I left the medical school to open my private practice, my new question was, *"Why do people get sick?"* I have found that when I am with a patient, and ask myself, "Why is this person dis-eased?" I can create new possibilities for healing and curing. As a result, I have witnessed countless "miracles."

The body-mind-spirit connection is such an important aspect of medicine. In 1985, I took an oath: "First, do no harm." Sometimes physicians will do the worst thing for their patients by taking away their hope. But even if there is no treatment, there is always hope.

In medical school, we received very little training in the power of the mind and how to use it. We never really looked at it as a tool to use in health care. Yet I believe there's never been an illness that could not be cured. It could be AIDS, cancer, rheumatoid arthritis or autism. People have been cured of these conditions or diseases. A specialist might say, "We misdiagnosed you—that's why you don't have xyz disease anymore." However, some of us would consider these recoveries a miracle. These patients know a healing took place, even if their doctors do not acknowledge it. These patients did something different. They expected a miracle.

I have proven "to think is to create" many times and observed patients doing the same. I know with absolute certainty that intention is the most important part of creating a dream. The mechanism will appear to accelerate the intention, creating opportunities you may never have seen or dreamed of. Everything is created from one-hundred-percent intention. Everything is created from what you are thinking!

If you want something, think it. Imagine it in great detail, full of life and color. Then get your doubts, fears and disbeliefs out of the way, and give yourself over to the creative power of your dream. Expect a miracle!

Curtis Takemoto-Gentile, MD, is a Native-Hawaiian physician currently in private practice in Honolulu. He sees patients of all ages, from newborns to centenarians. His practice is a nontraditional one, integrating natural therapies including nutrients, enzymes, probiotics, Chinese herbs, homeopathic remedies and environmental and energy medicine. Since opening his private practice, he has been voted Best Doctor of Hawaii several times. Dr. Takemoto-Gentile recently finished his first book, Optimal Health Naturally: What Your Doctor Didn't Tell You and Your Mother Didn't Know. *Connect at www.DoctorCTG. com.*

Kimberly O'Connor

SUFFERING IS OPTIONAL

I sit on the edge of my sailboat with my butt maybe two inches above the water, holding the rudder. The boat is keeled hard and we're flying over the clear mountain waters of Lake Dillan high in the Rocky Mountains above Denver, Colorado. I feel the wind in my hair, the spray in my face, and I'm free. I'm light; I'm filled with powerful anabolic energy and feeling absolute joy!

But it hasn't always been this way. Once I was trapped in a life dominated by soul-sucking, dark, catabolic energy. I felt obligated to a marriage that drained the life from me. My work was so demanding, so completely crazy, that I dreaded going to work each day. I would wake up in the morning feeling depressed. Some mornings I wasn't able to keep my makeup on because I would cry during my drive to work and wipe it all away.

Determined to please and to do the best job I could, I abandoned the important aspects of my life. Years of working at a demanding job in a "churn and burn" accounting department, with ridiculous expectations of time at work—late nights, weekends—devoured my personal life.

When I had down time, the phone would ring and I wouldn't want to answer it. It would either be someone from work or a friend reaching out; it was embarrassing to continue making excuses about why I didn't call back or make it to the dinner with friends or stop by the party that had been planned for months. I missed my own birthday celebration, for heaven's sake!

My niece and nephew, whom I adore and who live just around the corner, would call on a Friday to ask, "Are you working this weekend? Could we come over and see you?"

I rarely, rarely could make time for them. Even my dog got used to me not being around; Penny Lane was more attached to my sister Stacey, who would take her for a couple of walks each

We are all meant for greatness.

day while I was at work. I paid people to clean my house, prepare meals and do my yardwork. Stacey would run my errands since I could never make it to the dry cleaners or a pharmacy during store hours. I was a hamster on a wheel, running, running, running in circles with no destination in sight, and I was exhausted.

My life was consumed in this draining, catabolic energy where there was nothing more to life than working hard and long hours every day, never getting it all done, not getting appreciation and believing that what I'm doing makes not a bit of difference to the world. I had NO fulfillment in my life, no honorable purpose, and was hopeless about getting out of this cycle. I gave myself away to this job and this company and they ate it up and wanted more every day. My body ached under the stress; my soul was empty because it had not been filled up in many years—neither at work nor at home. Soon, there was nothing left of me. When I arose in the morning and hardly recognized myself in the mirror, I realized the Kim I knew was long gone. I had to make a change, or die.

And now, in my free time, I am a skipper, a sailor on a lake in the Rockies, filled with the bliss of letting go and the unity of my power and the power of the boat and the wind. Today my life is so full! I choose what to do every day. Maybe I'll have coffee with Mom or hang out with my brothers for lunch. I spend time with friends and am in close contact with my loved ones around the country. I walk Penny Lane and tend my own flower beds. I travel. I am of service in my community. I've returned to school to become an International Coaching Federation (ICF) certified coach.

Before, I never had a job that I truly loved. Now I'm an entrepreneur helping people get past whatever keeps them down, especially at work. Now I coach individuals and organizations on leadership, helping them to raise their consciousness by teaching basic principles of compassion, cooperation, acceptance, service, personal responsibility, non-judgment and reconciliation as well as the knowledge that everyone is perfect, everyone brings their unique gifts to this world and to the workplace. I enjoy both total freedom and total appreciation for me being me.

Each of us has a gift, and our
purpose is to give that gift away.

How did I reach this place of passion, creation and lighter energy? Suffering is not necessary; it's a signal from Spirit that you are out of alignment. Every day, I used the calm of meditation to create conscious contact with my higher powers. I used this opportunity to ask deeper questions of myself and of Spirit, such as "What is my purpose in this life?" and "Am I surrounding myself with people and organizations that support me in fulfilling my purpose?" and "What is the next best thing for me to do?"

You're in a dark space when you feel uncomfortable, critical, preoccupied. You are not vibrating at a positive, high energy when you're unhappy, tired, sick; when you're often fighting in a relationship; when you dread going to work; when you've no energy to walk your dog, no time for your friends and the hobbies you love. In this exhausting space, everything is forced and you find yourself feeling like a victim.

When you identify an area of destructive energy in your life, instead of fixing it, accept it. Meditate. Get honest with yourself, get quiet and go within to find out where the struggle is and what to do.

For me, the message I received from meditation and from my all my mentors and teachers was to move away from the negative energy. Leave it behind. Realize that you're bigger, greater, stronger and more powerful than this. We are all meant for greatness. We are not meant to be small, and in the dark, lower vibrations, our power is very small. Move to the light, where people hold you up,

*It's easier than you think to live
in lighter energy, joy, bliss.*

support you and see you as the perfect being that you are. We are all meant for greatness. We are not meant to be small, and in the dark, lower vibrations, our power is very small.

I loved my husband, and still do, but our marriage was rocky from the beginning. I had to be small and "less than" who I really was to make it work. I worked too much and ate too much and drank too much in order to cope. Because I was committed to being married and I loved him, I didn't want a divorce. But after a couple of difficult, very painful, back-and-forth years, I realized that it was best for me to love him and not be with him as a partner. Being on my own gave me the space to be the best woman I could be, to live my life's purpose and share my gift with the world.

Sailors say: "You can't change the wind; adjust your sails." I couldn't "change" my husband and our marriage. There was nothing to change; we were both perfect just as we were and are today. Yet it was time that we both trim our sails and set a new course.

Follow your energy. If you're in a situation where you feel bad, where your energy is drained, that is your body, soul, consciousness telling you it isn't a good fit. Do everything you can do to get away and move toward lighter, more powerful energy, which is your life force.

In meditation, ask the question: "What is the next step for me?" In meditation you get in touch with the universal power that has all the answers. Spirit will tell you and show you what you're meant to do on earth and how great you'll be at doing it. Each of us has a gift, and our purpose is to give that gift away while we are alive.

Then I looked at my job. I looked for the activities in which I found the most fulfillment, flow, joy, pure passion—those facets of my work that were absolutely right on and in alignment with my gifts. Over and above my skills in accounting, what I truly was known for was bringing my heart, my compassion, my wisdom, my strength, my joy to the people I worked with. I was great at empowering others, coaching them to trust themselves, knowing that they had all the answers.

I needed to escape the confining label of being whatever my job title said I was. Leaving my job and profession was not easy either. I had put my heart and soul into it for twenty-five years! It took courage and faith to become comfortable with the idea of walking away.

But, I did the hard thing. I know that, when I'm acting from the truth of who I am, I'm attracting every person and opportunity

Your sadness, your suffering is optional. When in doubt, let it out.

that will support me on my journey. As I was told when I learned to sail and the wind dropped, if you don't know what to do, let out the sail; it'll find something; it will tell you what to do next. When in doubt, let it out.

Once you understand what's running—and perhaps ruining—your life, it's time to get to work. I had to recognize and delete the old messages that told me to stay married and hang on to a secure job with a corporation. My coach and my teachers helped me to get rid of old instructions that kept me stuck and in charting a new course that set me free. A coach will remind you that suffering is optional and that you can just let it go. Every moment is an opportunity to change your course, change your life.

It's easier than you think to live in lighter energy, joy, bliss. Use meditation and reflection to find your gifts, what you're meant to do, what you truly desire. Then let go of the "have-to's" in your life and move, step by step, toward what makes you feel light, joyful, eager: the "want-to's." Visualize in meditation the life that you desire. You'll find, as I do, that you are powerfully creating that life and attracting like-minded people and opportunities that support you.

Absolutely anything is possible now: a bestselling book; a romantic relationship with the man of my dreams; a career of purpose that allows me to travel the world, sharing my gifts and myself with others; a long, healthy life surrounded by loved ones; and sailing, always sailing, in and out of favorite ports while going ever farther to destinations I have only seen in my dreams.

Your life holds vast possibility. Your sadness, your suffering is optional. When in doubt, let it out.

Kimberly O'Connor, BS, MBA, is an executive coach, leadership trainer, speaker and author. A coach for over ten years, Kim is passionate about having a positive impact on people, emphasizing strong relationships and a balanced life including vitality in health and career. Kim brings her twenty-five years of professional experience, along with her beautiful spirit and warmth, to individuals all over the world. She lives in Highlands Ranch, Colorado and enjoys golf, sailing, travel, reading, writing, meditation and spending time with family and friends. Connect with Kim at www.Level7Leadership.com.

Jason Diebold

—— ○ ✪ ○ ——

ACCOMPLISH YOUR LIFE'S PURPOSE

Think about the most successful people you know. Take a minute and write down a few words that describe them. No, really, do it. Just spend sixty seconds on the first step toward the life of your dreams.

Okay, now that you have your list, see how many of those words describe attitudes. How many describe skills? I bet a lot more words on your list describe attitudes than describe skills.

And that's great news! Our attitudes, which we can completely control and even change in an instant, determine how successful we are. Not our pasts, our families, our circumstances nor even our skills, but our own conscious attitudes, have the most impact on how successful we become!

I grew up in Michigan, where my family earned just enough to stay off government assistance. Things were not as easy or as luxurious as they could have been, but we were proud of our lives. I spent most of my life doing what I thought my parents expected of me or what I thought would make them proud. So I got good grades, respected my elders, achieved in sports, went to a good college, got a good job. Eventually, I found a wife, bought a house and had a baby. I did all this on auto-pilot, following the Midwestern work ethic. But I never really felt super content and was often just striving for the next accomplishment. I now know that was because I was not working to accomplish my own life's purpose. Maybe I was working to help my parents accomplish their own purpose, insofar as raising a good son was part of their mission, but this work did not feed my own soul.

I kept on this path until it exploded in disaster. Nothing was ever super bad, but nothing was ever really great or happy either. I spent most of my seven-year marriage just getting along. Then my wife left with my son for a wedding across the county and just decided not to come back.

For the first time in my life, I did not know what to do next.

Those were the worst days that I can remember. I felt lonely, abandoned and hopeless. I stayed in an emotional and physical depression for some time. When I was bedridden for three excruciating days with a herniated disk, I reached a do or die point. I could go on suffering as a victim, or I could strive to thrive as the master of my own destiny.

For the first time in my life, I did not know what to do next. It did not seem logical to follow the path my folks would want me to choose, which had led me into this train wreck. Instead, I chose to look for guidance from a place I had not spent much time looking at. It was not a friend or a coworker, not a mentor or an advisor. It was not even my own logical, thinking mind. Instead, I looked into my own heart, peeked into my own soul and asked: What is my purpose? What am I here to do? From what would I get the most fulfillment? What contributions do I have to share?

Now it's your turn. Take a few minutes to ponder these questions and then write down the answers:

> ‣ *What would you try to do if you knew that you could not fail?*

> ‣ *What would you love to accomplish if you knew that failure was not an option?*

The answer is your true life's calling! It is what you were put on this earth to do! I won't lie and tell you that I was immediately inspired to write a book or start a charitable organization. I started small, with things I enjoyed doing as a child or young adult, things my soul could play at before it was trained to settle down and behave—like listening to music, reading a good work of inspirational fiction, playing hockey and dancing. What my soul longed for most was love and companionship. I truly did not believe that I was loveable anymore.

One evening, as I played video games, ate a plateful of hot dogs and drank my usual excess of beer, I asked myself, *Why can't I get a date?* The answer seemed pretty obvious. Not many women would enjoy these activities, or the sloppy mess I was becoming, and I wouldn't want to date such a woman anyway. I knew the type of woman that I wanted to date. So I asked myself a better question: *Who would a woman like that want to date?*

> *What do you want to be doing*
> *when your time comes?*

I thought this successfully-dating man would be fit, attractive, successful, kind, adventurous, funny and just fun to be around. Now that I had a "what," the "how" was easy! I picked mentors and I followed them; I emulated them and spent as much time with them as I could. I leveraged their knowledge and intelligence.

The first issue I decided to tackle was easy for me. I had tried several fitness programs in the past. Power 90 had worked for me before, and it only took thirty minutes a day. That seemed doable, so I committed to finishing a ninety-day round of Power 90. This was one of my first lessons in commitment.

Your confidence builds as you pick a goal, commit to it and follow it through until the end. Fitness was great for me, because I looked and felt better as I accomplished the goal. Since it was one that other people have as well, I could help them accomplish their goals too. I have a favorite phrase from Zig Ziglar: "You can have everything in life that you want if you will just help enough other people get what they want."

In today's rushed and hassled society, we all struggle with too much to do in too little time. Most of us end up becoming very good at doing little bits of many things, rather than being very good at any one thing. But masters do one thing over and over, focusing on the basics.

It is easy to become an expert in any one field. If you only spend an hour a day reading and researching a topic, in a few months to

---

There are no small contributions.

---

a year you will have enough knowledge about it to impress most people. In two years, you will have spent over seven-hundred hours on your subject, and most everyone will recognize you as an expert in that field.

I don't want to tell you what to study, but rather ask you what area you would love to become an expert in, and enjoy teaching.

> *What three things would you love to become an expert in?*

> *What three things would you love to teach other people about?*

> *Which of these could you potentially earn a nice income from as a hobby?*

> *Could you stay interested in it for a long time?*

I am happiest when I am open, present, grounded and enjoying the process of being instead of doing. Funny thing is, when I am being what I want to become, I ultimately accomplish my required tasks! One of my favorite quotes, from educator Horace Mann, might inspire you when you selecting your area of expertise: "Be ashamed to die until you have won some victory for humanity."

My next goal was to build better relationships—specifically, romantic relationships—to fulfill my desire for love and intimacy.

I hesitate to mention my relationship goal, because it makes me feel self-conscious and shallow. But it was my strongest desire. My potential soul mate is an amazing woman whom I met at an annual celebration for PSI World Seminars. She works as a successful singer and actress here in Los Angeles. She has been studying personal development for over twelve years and, in many ways, is a mentor for me.

I reached my fitness goal in only seven months, and have maintained a healthy weight and body image for the last five years. My gift now lies in empowering people through the fitness and health industries. I believe that life is full of amazing moments, and we want to experience as many of them as possible in great health. Now, I know how to help other people lead happier and healthier lives. I feel truly blessed to know what my purpose is and to be rewarded handsomely for sharing this passion with others.

The truth is that we are all going to die someday. None of us knows exactly when that will be. But we can control what we are doing at that moment and the quality of life we have when it comes.

> *What do you want to be doing when your time comes?*

Write down what you truly would be most content with, what would make you feel most accomplished, when this time occurs. You've already done the hard part: defining your true purpose. Putting that into action is easier than living on auto-pilot and not following your real calling.

There are no small contributions. Whether you decide to be a life-saving doctor or a person of great service in cleaning and disposal, you will have many challenges! You will have huge successes, and also what seem like big failures. You will have good days, and days when you do not want to get out of bed. You will have times of great wealth, and others when you must make do. Any career or mission will have challenges. So make damn sure that you are working on a goal that fulfills you! If you are going to go through all of the struggles, be positive that your goal is a cause worth dying for. Because that is, in effect, what we are all doing each day of our lives: expending our life's energy for a cause.

I truly believe that, not only does the universe conspire to help you succeed in your true life's calling, it will also reward you magnificently when you do it with a high level of integrity, joy and gratitude.

Jason Diebold has been a coach for Team BeachBody since 2007 and has won several awards, including Elite Coach status for 2010 and 2011. He also develops online tools and videos for Team Beachbody. Once addicted to caffeine and diet soda, Jason is now passionate about nutrition. He has been a member of PSI since 2010, and has staffed several courses and seminars as a volunteer. Connect with Jason at www.JasonDiebold.com.

Terri Anderson Wilber

— ○ ⭐ ○ —

I DECIDE!

As I pulled into the parking lot at work, I felt the familiar sinking feeling in the pit of my stomach. I was the customer service manager for a Denver, Colorado firm that sent nurses across the nation on temporary assignments. Every phone call meant another problem landed in my lap. I could handle that stress because I was good at my job.

Todd, co-owner of the company along with his wife, Deb, was another matter. Todd was the playground bully—grown up. A fitness buff, he delighted in making demeaning comments about anyone who was the least bit overweight or out of shape. He was constantly saying derogatory things to me, telling me I was lazy or stupid. Because of his snide comments and lack of respect, I went to work each morning filled with dread.

I have always been relatively naïve, in a good, wholesome way; I always try to see the good in everyone. Though I was miserable, I thought I had to just "suck it up."

Growing up in the Midwest, I was taught that you got a good job and you stayed there. My mother's father was a builder who would work for a while, then play for a while. He was ostracized and given a hard time for that. I certainly didn't want to be picked on the way he was. Everyone else in my family worked their ten-hour days, day in and day out, year in and year out. My stepdad actually got an award for working ten years without taking a sick day—no money, just an award.

If you were unhappy, you coped by complaining to your family, dumping all over the ones you love and drinking heavily when it got really bad. There were many days when it got "really bad." I'd call my husband Ray and ask, "Why am I working here?"

And he'd answer, "It's a good job and we need the money."

I didn't know how to stand up for myself, and I allowed Todd's abuse to go on for five soul-eating years. One day, enough was

Because of his snide comments and lack of respect, I went to work each morning filled with dread.

enough. One of our nurses had been raped in Middle-of-Nowhere, Arkansas. I'd told her not to go back to work and that we would help in any way we could. The company incurred expenses when contracts were broken, such as for moving and housing. A few days later, Todd told me to tell the nurse that she owed the company eight-thousand dollars.

Instead, I negotiated with the hospital and got our liability reduced, from thirty-thousand dollars to ten thousand. But that wasn't enough for Todd. He raked me over the coals in front of the staff I managed.

I sat at my desk in tears, asking myself, *Why on earth are you crying over some guy's opinion—an opinion that is outright wrong, not based in fact and doesn't matter anyway? Who told you that you had to stay here and be beaten down? You are meant to spread joy and light in this world and you're NOT doing that right now!* I called Ray. This time he said, "If it's that bad, just go. Don't worry about the money, just get out of there."

A dam broke within me and I thought, *Why do I need his permission to leave? I'm grown. I decide.* I felt a wave of relief and release come over me as I became truly aware: *I make up the rules for my life. I DECIDE! I decide how I allow others to treat me. I decide where and when I spend my time. I decide whether I'll shine brightly or whether I'll dim my light.*

It all begins with *awareness*. Awareness of what's working and what's not. From that awareness, the path to positive change is easier to identify. I realized that I was the one who gave away my power *and* that I could absolutely take it back! I have this little thing called *choice* that I was completely unaware of until that moment.

I had been working part time for the last two years with a friend who had a balloon and event business. Now I had the time to start my own business, supplying creative balloon décor for large and small events. So when Deb called some months later, telling me that my replacement was a disaster and pleading with me to return, I agreed to meet with her, knowing I would never work for her and Todd again.

At our meeting, Deb passed me a blank sheet of paper. "Just write down what it would take to get you back."

> *My choice was my decision about my own self-worth and what I deserved, and that made all the difference.*

I filled the page. I wrote down everything I could imagine that would make that job palatable, fully expecting Deb to refuse—and that would be just fine with me: Reinstate my seniority and benefits as though I'd never left. Give me a thirty-percent raise. Give me a corner office. Repay what I spent on COBRA insurance. Let me set my own part-time hours. I listed every outlandish perk and benefit I could imagine. And then, the kicker: I want Todd to apologize to me in front of everyone.

Deb read the list. Much to my surprise, she nodded at each item. Until the last one. "Apology," she said, "that's going to be tough."

I put on my coat.

And then she said, "I said tough, not impossible. Take this list to payroll. You can have it all."

I decided to take the job for three months, working part-time while I built my own business.

With my new awareness of my power to choose, I sat at my desk the next morning with a new attitude. Todd leaned on my desk and said, "It wasn't the same after you left. I never realized how many problems you handled before they ever got to me. I don't know what we did to get you back, but it was worth it and I'm glad you're here." It wasn't a full-fledged apology, but it was a huge concession, and he said it in front of everyone. For the year I continued to work

---

It's not that anything *is possible;*
everything *is possible.*

---

for him, Todd never said another derogatory thing to me. Because I respected myself and demanded good treatment, he was positive and respected me and my work.

I know I am highly intelligent and very hardworking; and because I was in an environment where I allowed others to diminish that, I was completely out of alignment and miserable. When I realized and acknowledged how bright and talented I am and chose to *live* and *speak* my truth, the decision to find a better environment was a no-brainer. As a result of being my authentic self, I have created the business of my dreams. It allows me to use my creativity and love of people daily.

As I wrote my crazy list for Deb, part of me thought, *This is outlandish.* But another part of me said, *I deserve this.* My conditions reflected what I was really worth, and what my job should have been from the outset. And I got it. That shows the power of choice, the power of creating a vision. In effect, I created the job I had hoped to have.

My choice was my decision about my own self-worth and what I deserved, and that made all the difference. Like so many of us, I stayed in a horrible environment because I believed *I had no choice.* I could not see my other options. Rather than responding, taking a time-out and looking at the situation objectively, I just reacted with humiliated tears. It frightens me to think of how long I might have stayed if Todd had not pushed me past my limit.

Too often, we go through life deluding ourselves into not seeing a choice. In every situation, no matter what, we have a choice. First comes awareness, awareness of the reality of our situation and of our power of choice. And then comes a plan, and action. Even a bad plan with action is better than the best plan with nothing done at all.

With choice, I'm clear that, when bad things happen, I won't just suck it up and ride it out. Instead, I call these experiences "trigger devices" that challenge me into positive action on those days when life seems to toss a few lemons my way. I'll plan how I can be proactive, to minimize the damage or maximize the good that can come from the situation. This isn't always easy, especially in an emotionally charged situation. But it is essential.

Our choices do not have to be either this or that. We can choose to have this and that *and* that. It's not that *anything* is possible; *everything* is possible. When I made my "crazy list" for Deb, I didn't ask for either a thirty-percent raise *or* a corner office; I didn't ask for either full reinstatement *or* an apology. I asked for all of it. *Everything* means: I get whatever I want. It means I can taste this and that and that and enjoy all of it.

No matter what, if you want it, if you choose it, if you are passionate about it, *everything* is possible. You decide!

I DECIDE!

Terri Wilber has always been a woman on the move who never sits still for very long! She is the owner and operator of Balloonerific Delivery, Décor and Entertainment in Denver, Colorado, a full-service event planning and event décor company specializing in balloon décor. She is also a talented florist, and has re-branded that niche of her business as Sparkle Event Design for those clients (mostly brides) who aren't quite as in love with balloons as she is.

A vibrant, award-winning balloon artist and face painter, Terri has been painting folks of all ages for the past nineteen years, and added balloons to her repertoire eleven years ago. She is a member of the Face and Body Art Association, the Qualatex Balloon Network and Balloon HQ. Her work is internationally recognized, and has been featured in two issues of Balloon Images.

Because that's not enough to keep her hopping, Terri is passionate about personal growth work and is certified in NLP (neuro-linguistic programming) and hypnotherapy. Terri also provides inspirational and motivational items through the online store, Starfish Inspiration. Her book for children, The Land of And, *shows children that they don't always have to choose—everything is possible.*

Terri and her husband Ray, her high school sweetheart, celebrated their twenty-fifth anniversary this spring. Connect with Terri at www.SparkleEventDesign.com, www.TrueConnexion.com or www.StarfishInspiration.com.

Giji "Gayle Johanna" Galang

○ ★ ○

CREATE PARADISE INSIDE YOU

I smiled at myself in the mirror. I was bald, and maybe my ears did stick out, but I was beautiful. Shaving my head was a drastic step, but I needed to take a drastic step after visiting my dear Grandpa Bill. He had shown me our family photo albums, and in picture after picture, I noticed a sad, somber little girl. That little girl was me. He told me, "I remember when you were two years old, I sat you in my lap and you wouldn't stop crying until I promised to pay for your plastic surgery so your ears would no longer stick out."

My family teased me, calling me *"pangit,"* which means "ugly" in Tagalog, and "Dumbo," because of my ears, and unconsciously I took those words to heart. This was normal, to poke fun at our differences.

However, a belief arose in me that I was in fact ugly, and unloveable.

My parents separated when I was a child, after which my mom moved my three siblings and me into my grandparents' home in San Diego. Because my mom was in nursing school, my new extended family—my mom's younger siblings, Uncle Jr., Lito, Manny, Joey and my Auntie Princess—helped her raise us. Mom did not have much time to spend with us or to be at many special events.

This was also the time when I began to take hula lessons. The hypnotic rhythms of the music, sweet smells of the beautiful flower leis and thoughts of turquoise water and white sand beaches all resonated with me, and in those classes I forged a dream of traveling, and living, in Hawaii. Somehow, Hawaii always seemed to be home for me, even though I had never been there.

My *kumu* or hula teacher, Auntie Kehaulani Wilson, shared stories of life in the islands, where *aloha* is a way of living. Aloha includes the essence of unconditional love, so far from what I

A belief arose in me that I was in fact ugly, and unloveable.

received from my new extended family. I dreamed that I would be with the man of my dreams and raise a beautiful family in Hawaii—my idea of paradise. In my vision, my life was arranged so that I would be a conscious presence for my children, and raise them to be happy and confident. I would make sure they knew their value, that they were loved, that they were reminded that they were beautiful.

Hula is so much more than dancing; the stories of the Hawaiian culture are taught through every movement of the body, and those who witness it are touched by the spiritual essence of the dance. Auntie taught us how to gather our materials with love, and that by creating our own costumes with our own hands, we weave in that aloha. She explained the meaning of each word in each footstep, each breath we took and each leaf and flower we wore. Auntie explained how we evoke the essence of aloha in our dances; it begins in our hearts. When I was dancing, I felt joyful, beautiful, graceful. I was centered and grounded.

To escape the turmoil in my family, I volunteered to join the Marine Corps straight out of high school. I thought: *The Marine Corps will give me a chance to travel and maybe even live in Hawaii.* However, just a year later, I was discharged because of an injury. Coming home to San Diego, I was greeted with more drama.

My older brother had developed paranoid schizophrenia and my family was falling apart. My father had abandoned us once again. I had a falling-out with my managers at work. Relationship after relationship seemed to be ending, all around me. Even the used vehicle I bought broke down.

Then my Aunt Carmi, who worked for DC Cordova of Excellerated Business Schools at the time, hired me as a temp. I eventually became a production assistant for the Money and You Program. The concepts and principles I learned were priceless— and yet, because I didn't consider myself an entrepreneur, I did not know how to apply what I learned to my life. This was the beginning of my journey of self-discovery and growth.

In Money and You, the positive atmosphere and room to learn from my mistakes propelled me forward. Our salesperson, Bob Dietrich, invited me to attend the PSI Basic Seminar he was leading. Excited, I said, "YES!" As a result, I learned many valuable

When I was dancing, I felt
joyful, beautiful, graceful.

tools that I could immediately implement in my life. I began to discover the behaviors and beliefs that were not serving me, such as believing other people's stories about me; and I discovered the tools that supported me, like the power of intention. This awareness gave me choice: I can now choose to tell myself a different story; I can create with my thoughts.

After the Marines, I visited Grandpa Bill and saw how deeply my family's teasing had affected me. As I looked at picture after picture of a sad little girl with her hair carefully hiding her ears, I made a vow: *I will choose a different path, of love and beauty, and surround myself only with those who are nurturing and who positively support me.* I decided to shave my head, so I would not be able to hide my ears—and then love and nurture myself. With each pass of the electric razor, I felt my love for myself expand and the negative thoughts disappear, until I was able to look in the mirror and say, with absolute conviction: "I am beautiful." *I will tell myself I'm beautiful with every glimpse I get at the mirror*, I promised myself.

When I loved what I saw in the mirror, I created a genuinely loving relationship. Ronnie Baluca, my best friend since I was twelve years old, was single at the time and in the ROTC to become a commissioned flight officer in the Navy. He loved the new me: bald head, ears and all. He wanted to take our friendship to a higher level, and asked me to travel the world and commit to

Fall in love with yourself; then all else falls into love with you and your desires.

creating a life of love and beauty with him. Without hesitation, I said, "YES!" I could allow other people to love me. This was my Hawaii, my aloha, the beginning of my family.

Ronnie took up my dream of living in Hawaii. But because of his flight school commitments, we moved about every six months for the next two years. Now that I loved myself and could allow other people to love me, I created my own Hawaii wherever we were. I listened to Hawaiian music on Internet radio and bought Ronnie aloha shirts. No matter where we were, I found a group of Hawaiians to dance with.

We used tools I learned at PSI World Seminars to envision our dream house. (We still use these tools in our daily life.) First, we saw the perfect end result: a single-family home with three bedrooms, two baths and a fenced yard in Kailua, within five miles of the Marine Corps base and costing $425,000. We created Hawaii screen savers, treasure maps and vision boards of our dream home to keep it in the forefront of our thoughts.

And then Ronnie and I were stationed in Hawaii. We staffed a PSI Basic Seminar and continued to work on our house-hunting goal, adding more and more details to our treasure map. I was so tired of living out of a suitcase! "We are adding moving into our house in Hawaii within thirty days to our goal!" I said.

When we were asked to share about our goal achieved at a PSI Basic Presentation, I announced, "Once we have our nest, our babies will come," not realizing I was one week pregnant. It took ninety days to close escrow on our new house. After that, more dreams on our treasure map came true—and it hasn't stopped!

We dreamed of buying our first home and living in Hawaii, and now we've created just that, along with three amazingly beautiful children who support us in creating love and beauty in our own paradise. Because Ronnie is deployed to other countries for six months at a time, I have been better able to appreciate my childhood and empathize with my mother and other family members. They were the village that made me who I am today, and I am truly grateful for their teachings. Falling in love with me has allowed me to create a wonderfully nurturing, authentic and thriving life of wealth and liberty with my family and friends.

Once I learned to love myself, I discovered the other opportunities that opened up for me. I had always loved photography and had organized "photo shoots" with my younger cousins and friends as a child. I'd taken photography courses whenever I had an opportunity. So I created a successful freelance photography business doing what I love, and leveraging myself through products and tools I've invented to support others in creating joy by photographing smiles.

Love is the key! Fall in love with yourself; then all else falls into love with you and your desires. Let love be the only thought or feeling you choose to create. It can be challenging to go for a goal when you do not feel beautiful inside your own skin. When you truly love yourself unconditionally, when you forgive yourself and others for mistakes and learn from all of them, the possibilities are endless. No matter what stories have made been up about you, you are truly the author of the script of your life. So choose your goal wisely, dare to dream big and continue on when you reach that goal. Growth is a natural part of our being.

You can create your own paradise wherever you are, once you are in alignment within yourself. Big ears, bald head, big nose, short legs, skinny arms, knobby knees—none of this matters. No matter what you look like, or how others perceive you, none of it matters; none of it is *true*. Why let other people's labels keep you from your dreams? Love you, love all of *you,* and embrace the paradise inside of you. Only then will you create paradise, all around you, in which to live and thrive. Aloha!

Giji "Gayle Johanna" Galang is a yogi, photographer, inventor and the author of Smile Passion: Creating Joy One Smile at a Time. *She invented Smile Pals, digital camera accessories. She lives in Kailua, Hawaii with her husband Ronnie, and homeschools their three vivacious, beautiful children, Siah, Rinnah and Jonah. Giji now spends her free time as an Hawaii Chapter leader for Kids for Peace Global (www.KidsForPeaceGlobal.org), and as a volunteer yoga teacher for children at Sunshine School (www.SunshineSchoolHI.org), a preschool founded in 1978 by PSI World Seminars graduates, that teaches many of the same principles taught at PSI Basic for Kids. Connect with Giji at www. SmilePassion.com.*

Kim Dozier

FINDING A TEACHER

For weeks on end I tossed and turned for hours, unable to get a single moment of reprieve from all the endless talk running through my mind a mile a minute. I was so lost; I had no idea what to do, and no one could help. So I did what every rational person does: I got up in the middle of the night, dropped to my knees and started yelling.

"God, this is crap! Fine, great, you broke me! Now get me a damn teacher, you S.O.B.!"

Empty, dark, lost and clueless. Just a few of the many words I could use to describe where I was. Usually, I could strap on my always-reliable survivor suit: Get busy, put my head down and work as hard as possible at anything—and I do mean anything—to distract me from what I was really feeling or dealing with (or not feeling or dealing with), from pushing in my business twelve hours a day to scrubbing every inch of grout in a bathroom tiled from floor to ceiling that looked like it hadn't been touched since the 1960s. I would keep at a task until I numbed out, or until the pain lessened enough for me to breathe. But not this time. This time, I realized that I was completely jacked.

It was like being in a room where everyone else wore black, I wore neon orange and still no one saw me. These feelings of isolation only increased the further I spiraled. Any time I went to my trusty mental toolbox and looked inside, all I saw was a bent screwdriver and a rusty nail. The cold, gray metal box contained nothing that I could use, and all I could think was, *Where am I? How did I get to this place? I'm the girl who always has it together.* Right?

My brother and I were raised by our mother and by various would-be father figures. It was the sixties, and a single mother was frowned upon, especially in traditional New York. My mother worked all hours of the day in order to support us and, though the stepfather Mom found for us was a really nice guy, he also had a really big drinking problem. I found myself filling the roles of father, peacemaker and good girl.

As I later learned, my upbringing was far from normal; but it was never boring. There was always someone or something to take care of, and my mother needed me to be strong—with my stepfather's drinking (something that simply embarrassed me, rather than being abusive) and my older brother's propensity for rebellion, there was no one else. Mom had a hard time if I broke down.

Growing up, my mantra was, "Don't feel; just do." Thus developed my "Secret Survivor Suit." The queen of "suck it up; just keep going; you can do it; nose to the grindstone" was born.

I learned to step up to the plate and take charge wherever I saw the need, and somewhere along the way, I decided that as long as I did the "right" thing, I would be loved and my dreams would come true. But then I had a bad year—a terrible year, with one crisis after another. When I believed I had found "the one" and it all blew up in my face under some crazy circumstances, my theory and my drive went along with it. The day came where being busy no longer worked; suddenly my box of coping tools was empty.

I finally hit a wall, and I had to ask myself, *Why? !&^\$#!@! What else do I have to do? Be? I have so much, yet I feel as though I have nothing!* Stuck in my own mind, I saw no way to get out of or away from my sense of loss and sadness. I asked myself, *I have everything. Why am I so unhappy?*

Before long, I was trapped in a vicious circle: Wake up. Eat my breakfast. Brush my teeth. Go to work. Try to make it until five, when I can go home and cry again. Rinse and repeat. Endless weeks somehow passed, and I continued to slip into a very dark and lonely place. My friends were all at a loss as to how they should go about helping. More than one of them told me that they were scared for me, and of my behavior.

The abyss is a nasty and humbling place. I had nowhere to turn and felt consumed by the pain. Over the course of every day, the numbness with which I awoke gradually faded into body-consuming despair. I tried to imagine who I hated enough to give this immense pain to—there wasn't anyone I could wish it upon. I was always attempting to follow the rules and do the right things. I

Suddenly my box of coping tools was empty.

couldn't understand how I could be in this place of heartbreak, this time with no way to fix it. I thought that there had to be something wrong with me. To keep trying and keep failing... I thought it was proof that God hated me.

The day after my midnight breakdown, I managed to continue my perfunctory approach to everyday life. When I stopped by Safeway for a coffee, however, and got talking with two friends I ran into, I blurted out, "Do you know anyone I can talk to? Because I'm losing it!" All I knew was I needed the perpetual ache to end. I had kept myself too busy to feel anything for so long that now I was exhausted in my bones.

The next morning, I found myself sitting on Leeanne's couch. Within two minutes, the tears flowed as I told her of my heartbreak and loss. Finally, for the first time in months, I felt that someone understood—that these things I was feeling were valid and true, and that maybe I didn't have to shove them away from me. Leeanne told me that I had to have my heart broken in order for it to open again. Less than two days after asking for a teacher, I had found one. And so, my journey began.

Working with Leeanne was pretty different. Yes, we went back to figure out where I had created my stories and beliefs, but Leeanne is a shaman and a strong woman who lives in connection to her spirit. That was extremely foreign to me. She had spent years seeking, and studying the Mayan culture, and before I knew it I had left behind the comfortable familiarity of her couch for a trip to Guatemala, to truly begin my spiritual journey.

Mostly, I was clueless. There I was, in a remote, Third World country, hundreds of candles burning before me as I knelt and prayed to receive something from God. I had asked for *the* teacher, and instead I received a busload of them. The first batch of teachers

I thought it was proof that God hated me.

were Mayan, not one of whom spoke unbroken English. I began to wonder if maybe there was something else, and one day, I decided to challenge the spirits, asking them to prove it. That evening I got sick, and of course attributed it to the food. The shamans said I had the "Spirit Flu." I thought they were crazy until that night, when I had visions of being cared for. In the morning, I drew a symbol from my dream that turned out to be Mayan.

That was the beginning of my emergence from the abyss, but I still had a long way to go. I continued to see Leeanne and seek more. A few months after I returned from Guatemala, my brother died from a drug overdose. He had struggled with addiction for a long time and mostly I felt happy that he suffered no longer. After mourning him and cleaning my house for five days straight, another teacher came into my life. While on a business trip, I met a couple who, after hearing my tales of woe, told me that I had to extend my trip and go to a class the following weekend. "PSI World Seminars." I had no idea what it was, but I didn't care: I was open to anything.

Staying was the best decision I could have made. It was the beginning of my toolbox replacement; but this time, I didn't pack the toolbox full. I didn't need to. When wearing my "Secret

Survivor Suit," I am in complete "do it" mode: I put my head down and plow through what has to be done. This is very useful in business, but not so much in my personal life. So when I let go of the armor of always keeping it together, I began to feel real and true connections to what was going on around me, and there was suddenly a space inside of me that was at something akin to peace.

Because of the mentality I held onto for so many years, I always believed that no matter what I achieved or accomplished in my life, I was still inadequate. As though I could never be good enough. I always had it pretty good, yet I still had trouble really feeling, accepting, or celebrating it. In turn, I thought that my bad feelings were wrong, weak and undeserving of my time—or anyone else's. I hadn't nearly lost my life, or suffered any huge, tragic and life-changing event, so what right did I have to feel so terrible?

Leeanne and PSI both helped me to see that this discounting of the validity of my feelings was how I slowly but surely dug a hole of hopelessness and void space deep into my heart. Always obsessed with the end result, with everything being taken care of

I know I have the ultimate toolbox to turn to.

and tied up with a neat bow, I found myself so addicted to the destination that I barely glanced at the journey—and so I never gave myself the opportunity to celebrate the joys of my successes and achievements. The roses were plentiful, yet I never stopped to smell them.

In the past, it wasn't uncommon for me to wake up thinking the bottom would drop out at any time and there was never an end in sight. Now, I give myself an hour at most to think that, and then laugh at most of it because I recognize that nothing lasts forever, neither pleasure nor pain. I'm amazed at how often people point out the changes in me. As a result, life is so much brighter. And when it's not, I know I have the ultimate toolbox to turn to. I know now that this is the journey.

FINDING A TEACHER

Kim Dozier has owned and operated a mobile women's clothing company for twenty-two years. From beginnings in the Los Angeles, California movie industry to her current base in Colorado, Kim has dressed and educated thousands of women, specializing in fashion advice and fitting all body types and lifestyles. Her passion is guiding women in creating the image they desire, and loving how they look in the process. Connect with Kim at www.RackandRoll.net.

Emily Monroe

○ ★ ○

BRICK BY BRICK

It felt as though I had run into a brick wall. Suddenly, the running I had been doing for years, all of the momentum I had been building behind me, caught up with me and I was left breathless.

Blessedly gifted, I had been involved in something all my life. Family, friends, sports, barbequed-chicken grilling contests, school clubs, music, church, horse-showing—the list went on. In most aspects of my life, I never stopped. As I entered adulthood, my drive was just as persistent as it had been during my youth.

But could I keep that momentum going forever? I learned my limitations the hard way. Everything I had been running from, including the truth of my sexual orientation, suddenly caught up with me and I realized how disconnected I was from my center, and my spirit.

I knew that I had to make a move and, in July 2007, I took the first tentative step.

With my first real teaching job—something I had been building toward for years—came my first house. I've always had a thing for projects where I could see progress happening before my eyes, and how exciting this venture was going to be. The structure and roof of the house were sound, but cosmetically, it was a sight to make one's eyes sore. You didn't want to breathe the air when you walked in due to the awful smell and the whole place was infested with cockroaches.

I'm sure most people in my life questioned my sanity when I signed on the dotted line, but all I could see when I walked in was what it *could* be. Somehow, I had a vision of it being gorgeous—all it needed was updating, revamping and a little TLC. I was going to take this run-down house and spin a one-eighty on it.

Soon after the purchase was finalized, I began the long and arduous process of gutting the house. Full force ahead, I reduced the bathroom down to the dirt on the ground; tore down walls; and stripped the place almost completely naked on the inside.

> *I was creating a whole and peaceful*
> *living environment; I needed to be*
> *a whole and peaceful person.*

Methodically, I brought my little house to its most basic and skeletal state so that, equipped with a little experience and a lot of passion and determination, I could start restructuring it in every sense of the word.

While attending graduate school, as teachers must, my nights and weekends became filled with ripping out floors, hanging new walls, and picking out fixtures. I skipped around a lot, doing small pieces of work to each room.

The more I worked on the house with my own two hands, the more I fixed the things that were broken or in need of replacement and nursed everything back to structural health, the more I realized that I needed to apply the same love and care to myself. I was creating a whole and peaceful living environment; I needed to be a whole and peaceful person.

As with the house, nothing would happen unless I made it happen. For too long, the house of my soul had been gorgeous and amazing on the outside, but a disaster zone on the inside. Rebuilding my house showed me that running was neither the answer nor even an option; again, a move had to be made, and I was the one who had to make it. This move would not be around the matters at hand, but directly through them. No one would—or could—do it for me. It was up to me.

Nail by nail, brick by brick, the transformation of my little house began to signify so much more to me than just remodeling a home. I could see the progress in front of me, and tick things off my to-do list; yet I was still facing down my own inner brick wall,

I started asking questions of myself, the tough questions that I had avoided for so long.

which seemed as impenetrable as ever. Rather than beat my fists against it, I started asking questions of myself, the tough questions that I had avoided for so long: *What am I doing with my life? Have I truly been expressing my authentic self? Am I creating the future that I've always dreamt of?*

With every nail I hammered and paint stroke I applied, I felt the energy in the house shift until it seemed to have a soul of its own—a soul that was intrinsically linked to my own. It was almost as if, seeing something so tangible coming to life, I was given a vision to which I could aspire. Each room of the house started to signify a different part of myself, and as I did small pieces of work to each, I felt the doors to those rooms within myself begin to inch open.

The guest room became the people in my life. The bedroom was myself: my intimate space, my dreams and my closest relationships, what was most important to me. The office represented my dreams and my career, my jobs and the goals I wanted to accomplish. The bathroom signified a spa, of sorts—if I didn't take care of me, I wouldn't have much to give to others. Finally, the kitchen and the living area were spaces for me to open up and connect with people, as I loved to have people over and entertain. The three things that were lacking in each of these "rooms" inside me were courage, confidence and certainty.

Eighteen months after I began the renovation, there came a night in the guest bedroom when I started to get a sense of the peace I was hoping to achieve for myself. This room was the first one I completed. I had finished painting the walls and windows, hung the blinds, put in new closet doors, added trimwork, replaced the carpet and put the wall ornaments and furniture into place. I stood in the doorway, taking it all in, and realized that this beautiful, open room was the state of being I needed to head toward.

I had a lot of great things going on in my life—and here I was looking at myself, wondering why I was so unhappy. I shut out a lot of people, closed myself off from allowing close relationships. While renovating the house, I found many tasks I could complete alone; yet the rejuvenation of my soul required a few helping hands. This was not something I was able to do all on my own, and I didn't have to. I was surrounded by supportive people.

My parents were not the first people I came out to; in fact, my first relationship was kept very private. After that, I told my best friend, a few other close friends, and my sisters. With every person I told, I felt a little lighter and a little closer to being whole. Each conversation made it easier to open up, but it was the conversation with my mom that made me feel the most liberated.

I love my mom with all of myself. I didn't want her to get upset with me, and I wanted her to accept me—and all of those fears were running me. I went into the conversation with her wanting us to be drawn closer together, not pushed further apart.

Being open and honest with her, and more vulnerable than I had ever allowed myself to be in front of another person, was like a revelation. I was the one who was upset, while she hugged me. Of course there were questions; but, with her, I suddenly saw I no longer needed to hide so many things about myself that were integral to who I was.

This was a turning point for me; it was the first toppling domino in a long line. When I started becoming vulnerable and opening up, I realized that, however terrifying it could be, it was something to embrace.

If I hadn't put my house back together, I couldn't have even attempted to put myself back together. As each room in the house came to completion, I felt a part of myself within become more and more at peace. I continued to reach out for support from friends and family, and to reach out for God's guidance. To suddenly be walking around without all of the weight of my secrets and self-denial made me truly feel, in moments, like Bambi: shaky, wobbly. Sometimes I was unsure of what to say or do; but I had to accept everything as it was, learn from my experiences and make decisions based on the fact that I knew exactly where I was supposed to be and that I needed to live my life to the fullest.

In any renovation, the tiniest error can have a huge knock-on effect: a shelf hung not quite straight can result in the books sliding off the end; a roll of carpet that isn't quite big enough to cover the entire floor must be replaced; buying the wrong type of

> *If I hadn't put my house back together,*
> *I couldn't have even attempted*
> *to put myself back together.*

door hinge means having to go straight back to the hardware store. These errors happen in real life, too—and I began to flow with life. On my way home from a visit to my partner, I was told that my flight had been overbooked and I would be put on standby.

Something told me to stay. I listened, and made the choice to extend my travels. This one move sent my entire life in a completely different trajectory. The next day I resigned from my teaching job, and took a step toward my new career by attending a life success course. Within six more days, I was traveling on faith again and the ball was rolling. Aspects of my life needed to be shuffled around so that a firm foundation could be built for the rest to stand upon. And as my vision for my life grows, I must continue to expand my foundation when a room is added or an extension is made.

Thomas D. Willhite said: "To think is to create. To act is to achieve." Watching the house come to life before my eyes—and painting its exterior at a time when I felt like I was stepping into a new sheen myself—I realized that if I continued to envision my life and dreams without making a move, I would always just watch opportunities pass me by and go on to others. I could make life happen, instead of it happening to me.

To this day, the house remains unfinished. I once used it as a mirror for my growth; now I've freed myself from those walls and continue to expand. If someone were to ask me when I think the house will be complete, I would question, "When is a house ever complete?" I am less concerned with perfection, because it's about progress.

Emily Monroe, Executive Assistant to the CEO of Success Is By Design and The Women Of Global Change, is co-founder of Designer Insiders, a design and decorating company. She also has a degree in physical and health education. Connect with Emily at www.EmilyMonroeUniversal.com.

Jennifer R. Singer

—— ○ ✪ ○ ——

MORE?
BETTER?
DIFFERENT?

"What plan are you creating to make me want to leave?"

I stared at Mark, my new love, dumbfounded. *What? Make you leave? You're exactly what I've been looking for. Why would I do that?* And then it hit me: I was sabotaging my relationship, the very thing I had worked so hard to attract. In an intimate moment, I had just shared with Mark my deepest fears about our future. "This is so amazing, and I don't want anything to jeopardize this," I had said to him, looking for reassurance. His words cut right through me, and then I remembered: This wasn't the first time I set myself up to fail.

Growing up in Saskatoon, Saskatchewan, Canada, my childhood seemed perfect. I had a great father who provided well for our family, and a wonderful mother who stayed home and made sure my brother and I had everything we needed. Yet I feel that the pressures of being the model mother and housewife proved too much for Mom, eventually taking their toll on her body. For many years, she suffered with autoimmune disorders that caused her a great deal of pain, though she hid this from us, never complained and never asked for help.

When I was twenty-four, my mother contracted a blood clot in the stem of her brain just a few weeks after helping me pick out my wedding dress. I stayed by her side in the hospital, staring at her weak body, hooked up to so many tubes and wires. *This doesn't seem real*, I thought, even though she had been sick and suffering for a long time. Unsure of what to do, I went out to the waiting room and started to pray. I wasn't convinced that anyone was listening. Questions raced through my mind: *If there is a God, why hasn't He helped my mom to heal? Why is He taking her away? How can this be? She is the most loving person in the whole world! Why her?*

After discussions with the doctors and the family, we decided to cut her free from life support and help her make her transition. It was an unbelievably difficult decision. And yet, after she was

The more I feared what I didn't want, the more often it showed up!

disconnected from the machines, she seemed serene, somehow. And as a beam of sunlight shone down on her, it was if her soul was lifted from the body that had carried her most loving spirit. It was a very sad, yet surreal, moment I will always remember.

Shortly after my mom's death, I married my very own Prince Charming. He was good-looking, fun and generous; but even so, the years following my mother's death were full of extreme sadness. Sometimes I found myself sobbing so much I couldn't stop. I often let the doubt seep in; and, very quickly, my ideal marriage turned out to be very different from what I'd expected. As more challenges came up, communication was lost and we grew further apart.

It was a marriage full of ups and downs. We had a great time when things were rolling, when he was feeling good about himself and I piggybacked on that feeling. During those times, I had only positive thoughts about our marriage, and our future. But when things were bad and he was feeling low, I let negative thoughts consume me.

When things weren't going well between us, I often thought, *Would it be easier if I were on my own?* I imagined my life without him. *Would I be happier without him? Would life be better?*

The more I let my mind wander to these negative outcomes, the more challenging life became. The more I feared what I didn't want, the more often it showed up! Soon I started to believe that I really would be more at peace without him. I was scared to leave the financial security of marriage, but by then I had myself convinced that there was no other option. It was not planned; however, when our son was just two months old, circumstances separated us. And you know what? Life *was* more peaceful, and yes, I felt a sense of serenity. *I guess I was right. I am capable of doing it on my own.*

When we were living apart, my husband asked me to take a personal growth class, which, in hindsight, was probably his attempt to heal our marriage. I listened to the advice of friends and said no. Within a year, because I felt there was no progress toward our being happier together as a couple, I made the extremely difficult decision to file for divorce. After a lot of praying, I felt it was best for our children, and best for me. I wanted the kids to

> *For many, drawing negativity happens naturally. Is it natural to be negative?*

enjoy being with a happy mother and father—if that meant we had to be apart, then that was in their best interest. So many parents stay together "for the kids," but in some circumstances, that is not the best approach.

When you choose unhappiness and model unloving behavior toward your spouse, your kids may emulate this in their own relationships.

Now, looking back on that period of my life, and the events and circumstances that led to my divorce, I wonder what would have happened if I had been more open to growth, more willing to attend the class. I've since taken many personal growth courses, with my heels dug in deep, and these classes have helped me transform my life! Would we still be together today? I don't know. But after attending the classes, and taking a hard look at my life and my choices, I know for a fact that my negative thoughts, as well as the challenging circumstances that showed up *because* of the low vibration, contributed to the demise of my marriage.

What if, instead of imagining a life that was something more, better or different without my husband, I had imagined a life that was something more, better or different with him? Life is a *Choose Your Own Adventure* book, so I'll never know. But what I do believe is that everything happens for a reason, and people come and go from our lives for a reason, a season or a lifetime. I am so grateful for the lessons I have learned in the journey! I am happy with my life now and there's no going back, only forward. Still, I'm quite certain that we all would have had an easier time during the divorce if I hadn't given in to negative thinking. Now, as I focus on the good, I am truly blessed and full of gratitude to have a great co-parent who is a wonderful dad to our children.

When I was nine years old, my six-year-old brother and I were playing house when he said to me, "Jen, you are going to get married when you are twenty-five, have a baby when you are twenty-eight, and then have another baby three years later." I remember saying, "Yes, that will be." His statement, and my acceptance of it as truth, stayed with me ever since. I *was* married at twenty-five, had my

*When I change my vibration, I
invite all good things in.*

daughter at twenty-eight, and then, three years and two weeks later, gave birth to my son. Can you plan your life? Clearly, I did. I believed in my brother's prediction for me so fully, I thought of it often. Sure enough, it came to pass. And what I thought about what I did not want to happen with my marriage, that too came to pass.

We often talk about the Law of Attraction in the positive: We think, *I want to attract a house, or a new job, or a better relationship or a specific experience.* But we rarely think about the negative side of the Law of Attraction. For many, drawing negativity happens naturally. Is it natural to be negative? I now know that we can create a break-up just as easily as we can create a happy ending. Our thoughts create our reality; they influence our choices, the way we conduct ourselves and our actions. It was so easy to point fingers—until a dear friend pointed out to me that three of my fingers were pointing back at *me*. I am so grateful to be aware of this.

Even with all of my newfound self-awareness, even after acquiring amazing tools through PSI World Seminars and other classes, my subconscious mind still went to that place of, "Am I good enough?" This is how I ended up seeking reassurance from

> *If you want something more, better,*
> *or different for your life, focus on*
> *gratitude for what you have.*

Mark, the man who seemed to be "the one." When he said, "What plan are you creating to make me want to go away?" I had one of those big "a-ha" moments that helped me take ownership of all I created, the "good" and the "bad." More importantly, it helped me to have greater awareness, to stop indulging in negative thoughts and to change around any negatives much more quickly.

When you are operating in a vibration (the energy you give off to the world) that is low, you attract a bunch of stuff that's not so great. Have you ever stubbed your toe first thing in the morning, then burned your hand on the coffeemaker, then got stuck in traffic on your way to work, and found the day just spiraled down from there? Well, that's the low vibration I'm talking about.

Today, I focus on staying in high vibration and positive energy, knowing with absolute certainty that, if I do this, amazing things will come to me. The more I practice, the easier it gets. Whenever I feel myself in low vibration or think a negative thought, I redirect my energy and thoughts by changing my physical state. I get up out of my chair, jump up and down, put on a happy song and dance— whatever it takes. When I shift my physical state, my vibration naturally changes. And when I change my vibration, I invite all good things in. With the change in vibration, I was able to attract a great relationship, create synchronistic work opportunities and move from living in a one-bedroom apartment to living in a four-bedroom house.

And do you know what the best part of this is? You get to choose! Yes, you do! You get to choose which vibration you will live in; you get to choose which thoughts you will latch onto and believe to be real, and which thoughts are not worth your time. You get to decide that you're good enough, no matter what people have told you in the past or will tell you in the future.

If you want something more, better, or different for your life, focus on gratitude for what you have. Live in the present, focus on ultimate happiness and live without regrets. Don't worry, complain or fear the unknown, as the outcomes you fear will show up, guaranteed! Your life is your beautiful creation. Let your every thought support your bright, brilliant future!

Jennifer Singer knows firsthand the challenges of living a full and healthy life as a single parent and business-owner. Building on her twenty years in the fitness industry, she offers alternative ways to help people achieve ultimate wellness, and guides her clients toward ultimate abundance and an experience of health on many levels: financial, physical, personal and emotional. Her "FRENS" Wheel of Ultimate Abundance video download (www. JenniferSinger.net/bonus) helps people get unstuck and gain valuable tools for living balanced lives. Connect with Jennifer at www.JenniferSinger.net.

Bud Johnson

LIVING THE DREAM

What if you could have, be or do anything you wanted? What would that be?

Like many of you, I was raised by a father's iron fist. There was only one acceptable point of view in our house, and it was my dad's. The only power in our house was his authoritative rage and brute force. My dad was the god who knew it all. My feelings, thoughts and opinions were never considered. When I did express them, they were always slapped out of me or ridiculed. Sound familiar?

One day, when I was nine or ten years old, my dad asked me to go and get him a hammer. Off I went and opened up the toolbox. I dug around in it, but I couldn't find the hammer. I went back and told Dad, "It's not there."

"IT'S THERE!" he raged, and stormed over to the toolbox.

Why I followed I will never know. As soon as he lifted the lid, right there, glowing like a diamond, was that hammer. Right on top and in plain sight. What do you suppose he did? Well, he turned around and kneed me in the nuts. Ouch!!!

Yes, my parents lacked the ability to communicate effectively. And like many parents, instead of using love and understanding, encouragement and support, they—mostly my dad—continued to use power and control over me. For many years, I feared Dad's anger and the only safe thing for me to do was submit to him. I bought into his idea that I was useless and worthless, and I eventually gave up dreaming and expressing my opinions and feelings. Later, when I was exposed to drugs and alcohol, I ultimately saw no reason to say no. For many years, drugs would be my best friend. I had at last gained a sense of power—but eventually I blindly fell further into a prison of insecurity, self-doubt and powerlessness.

Well into adulthood, I secretly lived in a world of procrastination and felt too fearful to dream any dreams—especially the huge ones, the ones that would create the freedom to do whatever

What if you could have, be or do anything
you wanted? What would that be?

I truly desired. And when I dared to try dreaming, it seemed I would always sabotage any great ideas by very quickly allowing my fears to return me to my comfort zone with an excuse: "I can't" or "One day I am going to do it" or "I will do it tomorrow" or, the ultimate sabotaging statement, "Who cares, anyway." All of this, collectively, led me to a life of depression and an accumulation of unfulfilled dreams.

Many years ago, I was blessed with a moment of clarity that came in the heat of an argument, while I was trying to defend my stupidity. I yelled at my friend, "Well, what do you expect? I'm an alcoholic!" Bam! When I heard myself say those words, it was as though somebody hit me over the head. For the first time, I started to see who I had become and that I had been deceived by my friendship with drugs and alcohol.

What a shock it was when I realized I had been living an illusion; I was no better off than I was in my childhood. Only now I was the one not listening or communicating, the one who stopped growing, envisioning and accomplishing any realistic dreams. I had no points of view. The reason my feelings, values, thoughts, concerns and opinions were never ever expressed or acted upon was because now they were suppressed, shut down and ridiculed by me.

I had taken over my father's role in my own life, and although Dad quit verbally and emotionally abusing me many years ago, I was continuing to beat myself up.

Later, after many years of sobriety, my fears and self-sabotaging programs continued to prevent me from acknowledging that I was an artist. I felt ashamed to show my paintings or share my stories. One blessed day, Bob Proctor's testimonial introduced me to PSI World Seminars, and I made the decision to attend the Basic Seminar. I went on to complete the experiential opportunities PSI provides. Wow! It has been life-changing—full of insight, encouragement, guidance and inspiration.

PSI has given me the opportunity to actively take part in identifying my limiting beliefs. It has guided me to learn and accept that I am worthy of love and all that God has to offer, that "to think is to create" and that my thoughts and actions do create my own reality.

*I now believe that we all are worthy
of achieving whatever success means
to us individually, and that we can all
achieve it at no expense to others.*

I now believe that we all are worthy of achieving whatever success means to us individually, and that we can all achieve it at no expense to others.

Yes, folks, years later, well after the parental damage is done, children can learn how to develop the self-worth to find true liberty and create a successful life. But how much easier would it be if self worth came to children from their own parents' support and encouragement?

Just think, if my parents had learned some parenting skills about how to listen and communicate effectively, had they learned to acknowledge that I was of value, had they discovered the importance of guiding me toward dreaming and solving my own problems, I might have enjoyed a relationship with them. If I had been encouraged by these skills, I may have had the incentive and the courage to say no to drugs as a teenager. When was the last time you took the time to listen to or encourage your children?

It's amazing that, other than learning from our parents' examples, we get no formal training in how to raise children, communicate with them or support them.

Years ago, I took a behavioral parenting course with a dozen other parents. To my surprise, the first words out of the facilitator's mouth were, "If you parents don't realize that you're half or more

*I believe no one has to change very
much—but we all need to change a little.*

of your kids' problems, then its time to leave; don't waste our time." This allowed me to understand that my behaviors were affecting my child. Recently, I learned about Parent Effectiveness Training (P.E.T.) and am now in the process of taking a P.E.T. class in active listening and effective communication. Although they are grown up now, it will still benefit me immensely to learn how to better communicate with my kids, my grandchildren and people in general.

Despite the difficulties of my journey, I have been blessed throughout my life with more than the basic necessities. I am very grateful that I survived my dad's abuse and thankful for having stopped his devastating cycle for my family and myself.

PSI has helped me discover that I have the power inside to create a successful life and fulfill my dreams; to believe in myself and my strength; and to continually grow, create and nurture my vision of writing a series of stories for children. Springing from one of my oil paintings, the *Chirpy* series fosters a connection between children and their parents while encouraging children to dream and create results.

How exciting! My first book is being published and will be released soon. Yes, friends, if you are experiencing ineffective results in your life or relationships, you can learn how to change the old habits and programs. All it takes is to recognize that the current behaviors or relationships are not working and to know that it's okay to acknowledge it. Believe me, you're not alone. There's no shame in taking responsibility for getting the support you need to change and lead a successful life. Remember, God loves each and every one of us the same. I believe no one has to change very much—but we all need to change a little.

If you are like me, you will have to learn that your past does not equal your future and take on the process of allowing yourself to succeed. When you are ready to step toward whatever success is in your eyes, but fears plague you, help is here for you. For example, I encourage you to explore the work of Bob Proctor, Jane Willhite (PSI) and Dr. Miral Hassan (Universal Communication Skills), three valuable results-oriented resources.

When you learn to walk through your fears, you can be, do and have anything you want. Only you can make your dreams come true. So, again, I ask you to spend a moment and answer the question: What are your dreams? Then I encourage you to go out and create yourself an awesome life, my friends. God bless.

LIVING THE DREAM

Bud Johnson was raised in Vancouver, British Columbia, and is blessed with two children and five grandchildren. He is an artist and bestselling author who creates stories encouraging children to love themselves, confidently explore and think and create win/win solutions throughout their lives. Bud's first release of his interactive children's book series, The Adventures of Chirpy, *is due in January 2013. It is Bud's pleasure to invite you to follow his journey at his website, www.BudJohnson.ca.*

Mary Lee Newnham

───── ○ ✪ ○ ─────

A CASTLE IN THE WOODS

I felt the magical energy of the Sunshine Coast of British Columbia the first time I visited in 1985. The scenery of this paradise north and west of Vancouver is breathtakingly beautiful. The fabulous greens of its temperate rainforest made me feel at peace and in harmony with nature.

In Vancouver, I met my wonderful husband Michael and began a new career in the culinary industry. As my catering and restaurant business grew, I needed the oasis of the Sunshine Coast to take me away from the hustle and stress of Vancouver. There I found the calm and connection to the land that revitalized me and gave me energy to tackle my crazily busy life in the city.

Michael shared my dream of a getaway home on the Sunshine Coast. But it was a castle in our dreams. We couldn't possibly have it today. We didn't have enough money. We didn't have enough time. We would wait until after this, and that, and this again. But someday, someday, we would build our castle.

Finally, I bought a piece of land on the Sunshine Coast, where Michael and I planned to camp. We bought the land from a family who had camped on it for many years. The parents of this family had planned to build their retirement home there, someday. They had selected the right spot and cleared the land, but never built.

The father retired at long last, and was dead two months later. Their someday had never come.

Were we going to just hang on and wait for the right time to build, until finally we were dead, too? That possibility galvanized us. It wasn't easy, but I found an architect and, at last, we had the plans.

Of course, we still had doubts. *Was this really the ideal spot? Would we really be happy here? Where would we find the money?* But by now, we had both taken PSI World Seminars; and we knew that dreams can only become real when one acts on them.

We couldn't find a builder in Vancouver who was willing to work up on the Sunshine Coast. And on the Coast, alas, alack, no builders were interested in taking on a custom home, especially one with the insulated, poured-concrete foundation we wanted for energy efficiency.

Months went by as we diligently searched the Internet, home shows, building supply places—everywhere we could think of. Finally, Michael said, "I just know that if we drive there, we will find our builder. And we won't find one unless we go."

My parents, who wanted to share our castle, just happened to be visiting that week. The four of us loaded up the van, took our plans and set forth.

Believing is the big thing. But we didn't just sit and dream. We demonstrated our belief through action.

Believing is the big thing. But we didn't just sit and dream. We demonstrated our belief through action.

When we got into the area, Michael found a site under construction. He spoke with the equipment operator, who knew of a contractor who worked with insulated concrete forms and was working in a new subdivision nearby. The operator couldn't remember his full name, but the last name was something like "Badly." Michael and I laughed—sure, "Badly-built homes" sounded like the right guy for us. We drove over and found Ron Badley constructing a beautiful new home.

Michael spoke with him enough to pique his interest. He thought we had a great plan. After some discussion, he agreed to come look at our site. He was a few months from finishing the house he was working on and had not been looking for a new project. Ron said he had sworn off custom builds unless the house was interesting, the site was beautiful, and the people were nice. And we had all three! We were in.

But—and it was a major but—Ron did not work with budgets. He worked on a cost-plus basis; we would pay for all the materials plus a fixed percentage. We wouldn't know one month what we would have to pay the next month.

So we took not just a step, but a leap of faith. We'd learned in our PSI seminars that money is not a limitation. When you believe, and act toward your dream, the money will appear. And it did.

> *When you believe, and act toward*
> *your dream, the money will appear.*

Sometimes when a hefty bill came, we'd tell each other that we should have asked Ron to stop last month. But we kept going, and the money kept appearing.

Our friends told us we were crazy, that we were working ourselves into such a state of exhaustion that we'd be dead before our house was finished. We had our own recurring doubts, too.

Michael comes from abundance and is strong on creativity. I always believe that I can do whatever I plan to do. Because we both had a clear vision, our synergy made it exponentially easier to keep moving forward. We had no second-guessing, because we were both looking for the same outcome. Whenever one of us faltered, the other would carry on.

We kept our focus on what was in front of us, but we had set the map. We had intersections, detours and roadblocks along the way—that's life. Intersections were easy choices because we had plotted our course. We kept on believing and pushed through all obstacles.

At last came our first night in our castle. The exterior was up, the roof was on and the interior rooms were framed. We stayed in our bedroom, its inside walls covered with plastic sheeting for warmth and a mosquito net hung over our inflatable bed for protection. The haunting calls of loons on the lake woke me early in the morning. Through the holes where windows would soon be, I looked at the luxuriant rainforest and the lake beyond.

*It's fine to dream, but to make it real
you have to stop staring at your
vision board, put your shoes
on, get in the car and go.*

Pinch me! Am I dreaming, or has this really happened?

Our beautiful coast cottage is now a wonderful reality, a great place to escape and dream of our next big moves. So many aspects of my castle connect me to the earth, to my past, to my family.

Stanley Park, in Vancouver, is a very large near-wilderness area. I've always loved walking its trails. One year a storm uprooted trees over huge areas of Stanley Park. After a lot of controversy, the city found a contractor to take the fallen lumber and mill it into flooring. By chance, I saw the sign for Stanley Park Fir Flooring while driving one day. I had to have it. Now I have fir from Stanley Park flooring my dining and living areas, and the whole upstairs. I hadn't known that my grandparents' house had fir flooring upstairs. Walking on my fir flooring is like walking in my grandparents' house.

When I was nine, I went with a family friend, whose father was a forester, to stay in a forestry log cabin with a compact dirt floor. We played house there. While I was sweeping, I thought, "One day I'll have a house with a dirt floor." As I swept the slate tiles in my castle kitchen one day, it dawned on me that this *was* a dirt floor—just a little more solid.

The cedar on the outside of my castle, the fir trim around its windows and doors, its beams—all of it came from trees cleared from the land upon which it stands.

My dream castle is now a solid reality. I now know how powerful vision can be, how much you can create if you just start taking the steps. I've learned that the mind can't tell the difference between what we see as real and what we imagine. If you put a picture into your mind, all the power—every atom in the universe—aligns with it because, if you see it, it must therefore be real. Your mind does this whether you realize it or not.

As Henry Ford said: "Whether you think you can, or you think you can't—you're right."

It sounds simple, but it's hard to actually do. You have to put action behind belief. You can live in your dream and stay safe. It's scary to actually make a move toward it. You may have doubts. Taking action means committing to your dream.

It's fine to dream, but to make it real you have to stop staring at your vision board, put your shoes on, get in the car and go. Every step makes the belief more powerful. Every action you take makes the energy around that belief more concrete, because you are taking a step into a physical thing, not into thin air.

It's like using your headlights while driving at night. You don't see the whole landscape ahead of you, but you see all you need to see, and you will get there.

A CASTLE IN THE WOODS

Mary Lee Newnham is one of the premiere catering chefs in Vancouver, and has cooked for such luminaries as Queen Elizabeth II, Bill Gates and The Rolling Stones. In 1987, Mary Lee followed her passion and left a successful career in accounting and finance to pursue her love of the culinary arts. After graduating from Pierre Dubrulle Culinary School, she earned the position of chef and operating manager for the Petro Canada Executive Olympic Hospitality Suite during the 1988 Calgary Winter Olympic Games. She spent the next ten years working as a corporate, executive and private chef in a variety of restaurants, hotels, yacht charters and convention and conference centers. After leaving her executive chef position at The Atrium Hotel and Plaza Catering, Mary Lee opened Emelle's Catering in 1999.

Mary Lee is very dedicated to giving back to the community. As a member of University Women's Club, she has served as a frequent volunteer, particularly for Christmas at Hycroft Mansion. Further, she has worked as a mentor for young women at the YWCA and volunteers at Covenant House. She is currently writing a cookbook. Connect with Mary Lee at www.Emelles. com.

Todd Clarke

KNOW YOUR SUPERPOWERS

I'm a longtime freedom fighter—independent, fleet-of-foot, a traveler and an adventurer. I studied business in college, then redefined myself from a sales dude to a tech guy and switched to computers. After locking myself up in Sacramento for seven months studying programming, I pointed my carcass north to Seattle and got a job at Microsoft.

It probably doesn't come as a surprise that I never planned on having children. But my wife really wanted to have a child, and so I agreed. While we were pregnant, people would ask me if I was excited and I'd say, "I like kids, but babies? Call me when they're three, four, five. I don't care about babies."

And then the day they were born—"Oh my god, Babee, there's a knee, here comes one!" Three minutes later… "Here comes the other one!" Next thing you know, they're in my arms, these tiny identical twin boys, and I'm a mess, sobbing over my beautiful babies. Who was born that day? My sons, of course. But also, a new dad. Someone who realizes on a MUCH deeper level that life is not just a dry run.

I enjoy reinventing myself. I think it's necessary for people to do it on a regular basis. And I want to live an inspiring life for my kids. Being with them automatically focused me on what was really, truly important. So when they came along, I asked myself again, "What do I really want out of life? What am I really great at? What am I passionate about doing? Who do I want to *be*?" I came to the conclusion that I was just renting out my mind versus making a difference.

More than that, I realized that when my kids come to me and say, "Dad, I want to be able to do this, or that," I will root for them—because *I* did *what I wanted to do*, not because I *wanted* to, but

---

What do you remember doing as a kid that you could do for hours and hours and be in the zone? Do it!

---

never tried. I thought, *How can I encourage them to do something great, or unexpected, if I don't set an example for them?* So I quit my job.

In the months after I quit, I'd often find myself, crashed out on the floor next to my babies' crib, overwhelmed and thinking, *Who am I to quit my job and do this crazy stuff?* I'd wake up in the middle of the night in a sweat and talk myself through the worry. *Stop watching TV in the middle of the night to take your mind off this. Talk to the lizard brain. Tame it.* Talking out loud to it made the lizard brain go away.

I started doing a lot of reading and blogging about what was important to me. I read a fantastic book called *Unique Ability: Creating the Life You Want,* by Catherine Nomura, Julia Waller and Shannon Waller. The authors say there are four different kinds of activities we do: the unique things that give us tons of energy; the things we're excellent at but that *don't* give us a whole lot of energy; the things we're competent at; and the things we're incompetent at. The idea is to avoid doing the last three, even the things we're excellent at.

So I took an inventory of all the activities I did during the week and ranked them in those categories. I came up with a shortlist of the things I love to do and get energy around—my superpowers: facilitating group discussion; connecting with people immediately;

having honest talks; and making order out of chaos. The last thing I had on my list was "making things pretty." I don't know where that came from, but it's also always been true! I decided I would make sure to operate in those areas as much as possible.

Last fall, I attended PSI World Seminars. In one exercise, we imagined, "If I could do what I wanted to do, here's what it would look like," and wrote it down. Then we sat in the middle of our little subgroup and repeated it in front of each other, like a mantra, so it could start to become part of us. Seconds before it was my turn to go, this new idea hit me right smack in the face: *The world is waiting for my biz-art (artistic imagery with a business bent)!* It felt so strong, I thought, *I gotta do this. It had to come for a reason.*

So I started making these edgy, art-spirational images. I loved it! It took over, to the point where I made the out-loud commitment to making an image a day for 365 days. I don't know where they come from, but they just keep coming. As I said, I'm not a graphic

You make monumental, *superhero-sized*
gains when you build on strengths.

artist; I'm just a dude who decided to do this thing that excited me to the heart and cranium—immediately. And I am riding high with flow when expressing my business ideas with art-i-tude. In every way I can, I keep adding art to business, helping other people get that same exhilaration I got when my idea struck in that seminar: *Whoa,* this *was buried in me!*

What do you remember doing as a kid that you could do for hours and hours and be in the zone? Do it! It's our right to live with passion and our responsibility to find it. Don't waste another moment ignoring your superpowers. Do the things you'd happily plug away at, all day, for free. When you find out what they are, do the work and just keep going. No one can talk you out of it. It's non-negotiable. And it *will* work.

In business, at the end of the corporate year, you'll get a review: "Here's what you did well with, and here's what we want you to work on." Forget that! If you see a fault, ask yourself: *Is this something I really need to fix, or do I just imagine I do?* Maybe, if you were just operating on strengths and focusing on what is really important to you, that thing you "need to do" wouldn't even come to mind. Build on strengths and forget about weaknesses. If you work on a weakness, all you get are incremental gains—and what you end up with is a strong weakness. You make *monumental*, superhero-sized gains when you build on strengths.

When you understand what you're good at, you just want to do it. It doesn't feel like work, so you won't have to be poked and prodded to get things done, you'll just be intrinsically motivated. You'll write the papers; you'll do the research; you'll put in the hours, because you're well-LIT and full of confidence, and you

---

A little bit of targeted workplay each
day ends up accomplishing a lot.

---

want more of feeling so alive! If you have high skills and are unmotivated, you're bored. If you have motivation but not the right skills, you live in anxiety. It takes work to get to that confluence of skill plus motivation, but it's the only way to go. It's the way to enjoy every day and what we do.

In order to have a few good ideas, we've got to have a *lot* of them. They *should* sound crazy—we piggyback on those crazy ones to get to the good ones. Let's create a culture that supports that unique fire under every butt.

Business *needs* us to bring our art—our*selves*—to the workplace and inspire other people with it. I hear people in the elevator say, "TGIF," I'm like, "Yeah! Only two more days until Monday!" Let's love our work. Let's blur the lines between work and play. I fantasize about a culture where we link our g(enius) spots together, and everyone is operating with a smart-on for what they really care about.

Whip out a piece of paper and draw a line down the center. Label the top left "work," and the top right "home." Throughout the day, go to this piece of paper and write one-liners about the activities you're doing, like, "I wrote some programming code." "I performed some project management tasks." "I went to a meeting." Do that for a week, so you have an activity inventory of your life. Then start ranking these activities according to those four levels: unique, excellent, competent, incompetent. From it, make a really short list of your superpowers: what you're really great at and love to do in this life.

Keep that shortlist in front of you, and use it throughout the day to focus on what you love and offload what isn't important. Let's focus on less to get more done! It's about *intending results*. Define "done" each morning by writing what you will accomplish on a three-by-three sticky note. This is not your task list. This is your *accomplishment* list. A finite-sized list on a finite-sized tool for a finite-sized day. By keeping it small, you can prioritize. A little bit of targeted workplay each day ends up accomplishing a lot.

In focusing on your strengths every day, you're building something, creating something. It's an inner-cise in receptivity. You're not just trying to manage your time, get the project done or get through your day without going crazy; you're focusing on your strengths, rooted in passion, so you can be filled with the fire of creation every day. Even when you get frustrated, keep your commitment to live inspirationally.

It's your life, and your life depends on it. Don't be afraid to commit to your strength and passion—the how will work itself out. It's the *what*—what is it I really want out of life? How powerful do I want to be?

In February of 2012, I made a commitment to create one biz-art image a day for 365 days. Period. Why? For my boys, to show them they be great, that they can shoot for the moon, and even surpass it; that they can live a life without barriers. And for me, to show *myself.*

Todd Clarke is a coach, consultant, software developer and artist whose company, Get Lit, helps "light a fire under every butt" and build a culture of passionate excellence. Todd does what he does to recognize that the mundane is insane and the outrageous contagious; to be different; and to connect with and inspire others to be cool by doing more of what really, really matters. Connect with Todd and check out his Project 365 images at www.FireUnderEveryButt.com.

Shawn Robin Davison

○ ✪ ○

THE GIFT OF FAILURE

It was a nightmare. I found myself facing divorce after twenty-four years of marriage. Why did this have to happen to me? It was by far the most painful and difficult experience of my life. I didn't choose it, it wasn't what I wanted... or was it? I thought I was doing everything I could possibly do to keep it together. Why wasn't it enough?

My dream of celebrating a fiftieth wedding anniversary was lost. Somewhere along the way, I had decided that the ultimate marriage success was in reaching the golden anniversary, and I had become very attached to the idea. After all, we were almost halfway there. I imagined a grand celebration with lots of friends and family—grandkids, even great-grandchildren running about having a fabulous time, while everyone honored my wife and I for our commitment to each other.

Slowly, I finally realized I had to take responsibility for my part in this shipwreck, and there was a lot more to it than I imagined. I would never wish divorce on anyone, especially children, yet it turned out to be the biggest learning experience of my life.

My biggest fear in life was fear of failure. My biggest definition of failure was divorce. Having lived through my worst fear, not just surviving, but thriving in a wonderful way, I now have a new perspective on failure, and a new lease on life.

In retrospect, I see that I was committed to the game of marriage, yet was not playing to win; I was playing not to lose. There is an awfully big difference between the two. When things got really difficult and miserable, my fear of failure took over, and I became more motivated by my fear than by creating a relationship that would last a lifetime.

When we come to terms with our greatest fears, we are in most cases able to transcend them or move beyond them. Until then, not only do our fears hold us back; they can also become debilitating and often become destiny for those consumed by them. I believe there is a gift in every failure we experience.

Napoleon Hill said, "Every adversity, every failure, every heartache carries with it the seed of an equal or greater benefit." It's our choice to recognize and receive it. Although it was very difficult to imagine at the time that there was a gift and benefit to

I believe there is a gift in every failure we experience.

going through divorce, I now look back and see it clearly. Breaking through my biggest fear in life has created a whole new set of amazing opportunities and positive experiences.

For example, my relationship with my three children changed dramatically. I could no longer take them for granted; I realized if I wanted to have the connection with them I desired, I had to commit to being present, and really listen to what matters to them.

When my daughter says, "Dad, I don't feel like going to piano lessons today…" I now listen much better, and do my best to understand from her perspective. It's not easy, as my own programs are firing: "Push her—you're failing as a father if you don't push her," "You've got to work really hard to succeed," "We have a commitment to keep," "I still have to pay for it," "Blah, blah, blah." The reality is, she just wants to know that I love her and will support her, even when she doesn't feel good, and, as she would say, "It's not about you, Dad."

I am so grateful for the close bond I have with my children today—I am truly committed to win-win relationships, and nothing less. This has been both a personal and professional transformation. My business has grown dramatically by creating win-win relationships with my customers, who in turn generate referrals, which helps make my world go round.

In the game of life, I had to seriously lose in order to see how much I truly have gained. Many years ago, I was on a quest to get clear about my life's purpose, my big why. From all of the

> *In the game of life, I had to seriously lose in order to see how much I truly have gained.*

personal development and learning I had done, I knew having a purpose was really important. Dr. Hill said, "The starting point of all human achievement is the development of a definite major purpose. Without a definite major purpose, you are as helpless as a ship without a compass."

So I found my big why, and I was very happy about it, as it gave me great confidence to know I had an honorable purpose: to help bridge the gap in communication between younger and older generations.

More specifically, my purpose was to help older people share their most significant life lessons, while encouraging and helping young people to seek wisdom at an early age. Several years later there was still a problem. My *why* was so big, I thought of it as something that would happen in the future; it was something that I was working toward, yet was not ready to do—or, more importantly, *be.*

Having a definite major purpose was not enough. I worked very hard to create an amazing future, and then got frustrated when I thought I wasn't getting there fast enough. It seemed continually out of my reach; as if I could be successful if I worked really hard at it, yet not *really* successful. My business was surviving, yet not quite thriving. I was afraid of BIG SUCCESS almost as much as I was afraid of failure.

The big "a-ha" moment came from realizing in a whole new way that all we really have is *now*. I knew this in a logical sense, but something was different this time. I was in the bathtub, feeling sorry for myself, and it hit me like a ton of bricks!

I had been attending a PSI World Seminars Mastery Class, and the facilitator said in jest, "If you keep one foot in the past and one in the future, you're just pissing on the present." That was me! I

Life didn't have to look like the fully realized vision; the moment could be just a step in the journey.

was holding onto stuff in the past that was not serving me. I was so used to dragging this stuff behind me, I wasn't conscious of it anymore.

By accepting the gift of failure and realizing its benefits, I was able to let go of the stuff I was dragging behind me from the past. I also let go of that perfect-future fantasy and the frustration that came along with it. What I was missing was the fact that I could live my purpose now, in *this* moment. Life didn't have to look like the fully realized vision; the moment could be just a step in the journey. This was extremely powerful *and* practical.

Today, I strive to live my life with meaning, purpose and priority. I'm still taking small steps toward the big why, yet with each one, the bigger picture is becoming more apparent. I am connecting with the older generation and capturing their wisdom for my series, "Legends of the Human Spirit." I volunteer-coach on a periodic basis for a ninety-day PSI Leadership and Awareness Program. I have a dream to effectively communicate the Twelve Riches of Life, as defined by Napoleon Hill, to teenagers and young people around the world.

What is your big why? What small step can you take today to live your purpose? It's not that I don't have any fear of failure today, but rather that I have a different perspective, a respect for and faith that, when I fail, the learning and benefits will be much greater than the experience itself. Accepting the gift of failure does not mean you accept defeat or resignation. It means you have realized value from the experience, and the learning and benefits are greater than the failure itself.

Every Olympic gold medalist, every great author, every great leader—in fact, anyone who is considered successful—has had to experience tremendous failure before realizing ultimate success. For me personally, accepting the gift of failure was the key to realizing: I can live my purpose now. For many, accepting the gift of failure is the foundation and inspiration that drives their purpose in life.

When you look back on your life, how do you feel about the mistakes and failures along the way? Is there something you can learn from each experience that was positive, possibly really significant? Can you find the seed of equivalent or greater benefit?

Happiness is a choice, defiantly
shaped by our attitude toward life
and how we think we fit into it.

We are not the sum of our experiences, yet the choices we make as a result of those experiences define our character. I am no longer focused on having a fiftieth wedding anniversary; on the other hand, I have gained tremendous experience in what it takes to create a relationship that lasts a lifetime. Happiness is a choice, defiantly shaped by our attitude toward life and how we think we fit into it.

I have been "aspiring" to be a writer for many years. Again, it was something I thought of myself doing in the future, something I was working toward, yet somehow not ready to *be*.

I have stopped "aspiring" and I'm doing something about it! This book and this chapter are part of my personal dream machine. They are a small step toward my dream of being a great writer, enabling me to live my purpose now! I may fail miserably, yet I know without a shadow of doubt that I will benefit tremendously from the gift of failure.

Shawn Robin Davison is a serial entrepreneur with more than twenty years of experience building successful software and technology companies. He is the architect of software that is used daily by millions of people around the world. He loves to translate business and consumer needs into great products that make a positive impact on people's lives.

Shawn lives in Colorado, and his passions include family, photography, nature, health and writing. He is an avid snowboarder and kiteboarder and student of human nature and the mind. He is particularly fascinated with communicating wisdom and the energy of ideas. Connect with Shawn at www. ShawnRobinDavison.com.

Liane Uda

○ ★ ○

HAPPINESS NOW

"Everything's going to be okay, Liane," my mom said, smiling at me across her kitchen table. "I can beat this. I know it."

I looked at her thin, pale face with sadness. Before her out-of-the-blue diagnosis of stage III breast cancer and months of radiation and chemotherapy treatments, she had been so strong and healthy. Her cheeks had been round and rosy, her hair shiny and full. Now, even though she was so young, she looked almost old. *If something happens to Mom, I'll be lost,* I thought.

She looked like a shadow of her former self, but her spirit seemed to shine even brighter than ever. Along with the sadness and worry for my mom, I was filled with admiration for her positive attitude. *If she can stay positive when she feels this bad and when she knows there's a possibility she might not make it, I can stay positive too. Who knows how long any of us have? I have to stop waiting and start living.*

I grew up in a loving middle-class household and had a happy childhood. Everyone got along. My mom was a teacher; my dad was a salesman. We had everything we needed to survive and didn't seem to struggle.

I did wrestle with my weight and withstood teasing and name-calling from elementary school days till high school. Somewhere along the way, as I grew into my teens, I started to look at my relationships with boys as a place of safety and belonging. As I searched for love, sex was a comfort that told me I was valued and accepted. In my late teens, I was involved in quite a few physical and short-term relationships.

When I met Jon, I was nineteen. His attention bowled me over—he did all the right things and told me everything my low self-esteem was starving to hear. Everything seemed right, in the beginning. We had a great time hanging out together and spent hours talking on the phone at night. I thought we were in love. But

Then I found out I was pregnant.

after we dated for several months, Jon suddenly disappeared. He wouldn't answer his phone, and I couldn't find him in any of the usual places. He didn't respond to e-mails. It was as though he had fallen off the planet. I was devastated. *He told me he loved me!* Then I found out I was pregnant.

Weeks went by with no sign of Jon, as I tried to decide what to do about my pregnancy. Then I got a mysterious e-mail from a stranger, telling me, "I can explain some things here." *Whoa! Who is this?* "Jon uses people," the e-mail went on. "He's had a girlfriend for the past two-plus years, and he still lives with her. He cheats on her and uses other people for money or for sex. Then he'll just disappear." Though I didn't know who the writer was, her words matched up with my experience. I believed her. I was so heartbroken I thought about putting an end to my life. I told myself, *I will never trust a man again.*

Eleven weeks later, I made the difficult decision to have an abortion. I knew I was in no shape to raise a child, financially, mentally or emotionally. The day before the abortion, Jon finally e-mailed me back. His reaction to the news that I was pregnant was, "Well, what do you want me to do about it?" After that, I never heard from him again.

Going through the abortion was scary, but I knew I wasn't ready for a child. Still, after the procedure I became very depressed. It was not so much the pregnancy and the abortion that made me feel destroyed; it was that everything I thought we had was a lie. It seemed so good, and then he just disappeared.

From that time forward, I started relationships with this new attitude of distrust, not realizing they could only end in one way: disaster. I'd say to a new boyfriend, "I need you to show me I can trust you," but there was no way *anyone* could ever show me that. No matter how genuine love seemed, I could never get to the point of trust in a relationship. Underneath it all was the paralyzing thought: *You're going to disappear.*

As time went on, I pulled back from life in general and lived in a deepening state of worry, doubt, fear and sacrifice. There never seemed to be enough: enough time, enough money, enough love or enough certainty. So I was always in a rush to store those things up. My philosophy was, *Save and sacrifice now for the future, and one day, maybe, I will be happy.* I lost friendships because I worked

> *I didn't realize I was isolating myself
> and sacrificing my own happiness.*

constantly. Keeping in contact and meeting up with friends and family were sacrificed to more time for my jobs and school. I didn't realize I was isolating myself and sacrificing my own happiness.

Three years ago, I was introduced to PSI World Seminars by an ex-boyfriend. Around the same time, my mom was diagnosed with breast cancer. Taking PSI classes and listening to different speakers, I started to really get the message: "If it is to be, it is up to me." Feeling the power of Mom's positive outlook on her health and her family and getting a sense of how short life can be, it came to me that the way I was living was never going to make me happy. I would need to change things, so that I could be happy now and live the life I wanted to live now, not just "maybe someday"—or my life would be one of what ifs, regrets and I should haves. I was raised to have goals and to try to do something greater, and that's a good thing. But it's also important to be happy NOW, not just later.

It has been quite an interesting ride, learning how to let myself live and be happy. It's taken many moments of self-reflection and a lot of training and practice to change my philosophy of life, my way of thinking and my decision making. That work has been rewarded with the return of my self-confidence, my self-worth and the belief that I can conquer anything my mind dreams.

In fear, I held myself back for a long time. PSI taught me that I was operating from "not enough," versus operating from abundance. I've learned that "not enough" is just an excuse, and

*I can sacrifice, but I also need
to enjoy my present.*

my attitude, positive or negative, has a large role in the outcome of my experiences. I'm responsible for choosing which side to be on. I keep practicing releasing my past, forgiving both myself and others for what has happened, and consciously creating my present and my future.

After a year of chemo and radiation, my mom went into remission, only to find out less than three years later that the cancer had returned. The news was devastating. She went through more chemo, which didn't help, and now the doctors say she's had all the chemo she can take. We're constantly monitoring her condition these days to see if it gets worse, if the cancer grows or if it attaches itself to an organ. We never know what will happen next. When you think about it, though, isn't that the truth for everyone?

My mom's experience has taught me to balance my life. I can sacrifice, but I also need to enjoy my present.

You really do not know how long your life will be or what will happen. My own health issues—arthritis, bad knees and possibly inactive lupus—have made me even more aware that if I want something, now is the time to go for it. I've known many people with lupus who spend most of their time in the hospital. I'm lucky not to be there, and I am convinced that consistently making the choice to keep a positive attitude has helped me stay healthier.

Of course, I don't want to lose my mom. But otherwise, I find myself very happy and content. If something were to happen to me tomorrow, or next year, I'd feel very happy with what I've accomplished in my life so far. I make time now to do the things I want to do, like spending time with family and friends, traveling, trying new things or just taking time for me. I no longer feel as though I'm rushing to fill some hole in my soul while distracting myself from who I really am or what I really want to do.

With practice, every situation you come into—whether it be at work, with family or in other relationships—becomes an opportunity for you to catch yourself before making a decision and ask, "Is this going to be the best thing, or is there a different choice? Do I have a choice to react a different way and produce a different outcome?" Practicing that has made me a much more positive person. And the outcomes are much better.

Many people think that the way they are now, or what their current situation is, is all they are or all there is. But there's never only one option. There are always different options; it's just up to you to open your mind and make the choice. You can be happy— you may just need to do things differently, open yourself up to a different perspective or shift an attitude or old belief.

With that freedom, you can make sure to do what you want to do today in case it can't happen tomorrow. Enroll in PSI Basic Seminars. Write a bucket list and start living your dreams now, not tomorrow.

Happiness is possible, now *and* later. It is up to you. You are in control. You are the driver of your life. Own up to it and lead your life with confidence, love and passion in order to find true success and happiness within, not just outside.

HAPPINESS NOW

Liane Uda was born in Honolulu, Hawaii and lives there today. She is a marketing manager and world traveler with a passion for helping people achieve their goals, enjoying adventurous activities and trying new things. Her ambitions for the coming year include plenty of travel, learning to skydive and parasail and getting involved in the real estate market.

CONCLUSION

When I was thinking about the title of this book—*Your Dream Machine*—I immediately thought of the Basic Seminar, PSI World Seminars' "first step" class. You now know that your mind *is* your dream machine; the Basic Seminar is designed to help you harness the power of your mind so that whatever you can see, you can *be*.

In Basic, we go beyond the lessons learned in this book, and apply the principle "to think is to create" to all areas of life, including relationships, wealth, confidence, balance, creativity, productivity, memory and communication. Of course you could learn this information in so many ways—from books, or audio recordings or lectures—but I believe the Basic Seminar is the fastest way to gain insight and awareness, and to learn the essential tools and techniques for profound, lasting change.

If for some reason you can't get to a Basic Seminar in your area, start by reading Napoleon Hill's book, *Think and Grow Rich*. Read it five times, and then read it again. Bob Proctor is one of the finest teachers on getting your mind ready for success. Listen to his recordings; listen to them over and over again. Start with Proctor and Hill, and then find other teachers. Every book or recording that you see or hear about transformation, or success, or living a better life will move your mind into having something better, having something *more*. When you're ready, there will always be teachers; you simply have to be willing to hear them.

In our seminars we also teach the importance of living in gratitude. When you are grateful for all that you have—the good stuff and the challenges—more of what you *do* want will come to you. I've seen so many people cut off that flow of abundance because they weren't grateful for it, for all things.

Each morning, I wake up and say, "Thank you so much for this day. I'm alive, I'm breathing. Thank you for allowing me to live in a beautiful home, to have a loving family and fantastic friends. And thank you for yesterday's problems, too." And each night, I run through my day, and express my gratitude for all that came to me—the "good" and the "bad."

Being of service is also intertwined with "to think is to create." Just as lack of gratitude will stop the flow of abundance, holding on

---

This world has enough abundance for all.

---

to too much will also prevent you from truly living the life of your dreams. When you are in service to humanity without any thought of return or acknowledgment, you open the door to abundance— it's how you get the goodies!

Do you know the story of the monkey and the tree? Hungry, the monkey puts his hand in a hole in a tree, looking for bugs. He finds so many, more than he can handle, but he wants them all. When he tries to pull his hand out of the hole, it's too full and gets stuck in the tree. He's so focused on keeping all the bugs for himself, he won't let go of them. His hand will be stuck in that tree until he lets go. The lesson is, don't be the monkey! Don't hold on to things. This world has enough abundance for all.

I know all of my insightful, brave, wonderful co-authors share my dream of achieving world peace in our lifetime. I know this because all of their stories exemplify the principle "to think is to create," and emphasize the importance of never letting go of your dreams. Even when the dream is as big, and bold, and seemingly impossible as world peace, we must never let go of it. I also know that the principles we teach at PSI World Seminars empower and enable each and every student to help make this beautiful dream happen. This is my greatest hope, my grandest vision, my most important wish.

Right now, right this very minute, there are people thinking exactly as you think. Imagine what we could accomplish if we all held the space for world peace, if we all saw it clearly in our minds, millions of us, creating a vision of a peaceful world.

As you close this book, I could call on you to go after your dreams—but I won't. I won't ask you to do that, because I know that you will. I know that if you follow the principle "to think is to create," you will be well on your way toward living the life you've always wanted to live.

Instead, I humbly ask that, before you go to bed tonight, you give thanks for all that you have and that you picture a peaceful world, in perfect harmony.

Jane Willhite
Co-Founder, PSI World Seminars

ABOUT PSI WORLD SEMINARS

PSI (Personal Success Institute) is a company with a dream...a dream of a more cooperative and harmonious world where people are empowered to realize lives of liberty, purpose and passion.

In 1973, PSI World Seminars was created to spread the personal success principles that had brought the founders, Thomas D. Willhite and Jane C. Willhite, so much liberty in their lives. That same year, Tom and Jane also founded PSI World, an organization that coordinates groups of volunteers from around the world to work together in synergy for various relief projects. The mission of PSI World is World Peace One Mind at a Time.

In 1983, Tom died in a plane crash when his biplane went down at the company headquarters. Since that time, Jane has run the company as CEO and is responsible for its current growth and success.

For nearly forty years, PSI has worked with hundreds of thousands of people all over the world, helping them discover their ultimate effectiveness through breakthrough educational programs. As the oldest running personal development company in the United States, PSI is a leading authority and pioneer in human potential training.

Focused on optimizing the human experience by creating liberty in the lives of students, PSI strategies aim to enhance every area of life. The majority of our students have found substantial increases in the following areas:

- ◇ Dramatically improve communication abilities
- ◇ Enhance personal relationships
- ◇ Gain more confidence and increase productivity
- ◇ Discover more creativity, direction and focus

To learn more about PSI World Seminars, visit
www.PSIWorldSeminars.com
To learn more about PSI World, visit
www.PSIWorld.org

MY GIFT FOR YOU

I would love for you to have a free digital copy of Living Synergistically, *a book written by my late husband, Thomas D. Willhite. If you're considering taking our PSI Basic Seminar, this book is an introduction to the concepts presented during the course. In fact, everything in this book came out of the Basic Seminar.*

The PSI Basic Seminar has been a vehicle for hundreds of thousands of people to achieve their dreams. In Living Synergistically, *you have the opportunity to explore these same success principles in written form.*

As Tom says in the book, "People can become anything that they want to become. Everyone has the ability—all that is needed is the will, a plan and the power to put that plan into action."

To get your free download of this life-changing book, go to
www.LivingSynergistically.com

Jane C. Willhite

We invite you to experience the
Your Dream Machine
True Stories of Creating Abundance
MULTIMEDIA book.

Now that you've read these inspiring stories, you can also view the online version of YOUR DREAM MACHINE on your computer or iPad in an exciting, next-generation multimedia format.

Adding AUDIO and VIDEO conversations to the text, the co-authors share more knowledge and inspiration to help you use your own dream machine to create a life of abundance.

We offer you a GIFT of several chapters from the
Your Dream Machine
MULTIMEDIA book at:

www.YourDreamMachineBook.com

If you wish to buy the complete multimedia book, please use this coupon code to receive a substantial discount.

Coupon Code — Book10

We invite you to read and experience several free chapters of other Yinspire Media multimedia books. If you wish to buy the complete multimedia books, we invite you to use the coupon codes to receive a substantial discount.

Succeeding In Spite Of Everything

www.SucceedingInSpite.com

Coupon Code – Book9

Living Proof

Celebrating the Gifts that Came Wrapped in Sandpaper

www.LivingProofMBook.com

Coupon Code – Book5

Unbreakable Spirit

Rising Above the Impossible

www.UnbreakableSpiritBook.com

Coupon Code – Book8

Get Your Woman On

Embracing Beauty, Grace & The Power of Women

www.GetYourWomanOnBook.com

Coupon Code – Book7

Fight For Your Dreams

The Power of Never Giving Up

www.Fight4YourDreams.com

Coupon Code – Book6

How Did You Do That!

Stories of Going for IT

www.HowDidUDoThat.com

Coupon Code – Book2

The Law of Business Attraction

Secrets of Cooperative Success

www.LawOfBusinessAttraction.com

Coupon Code – Book1

Transforming Through 2012

Leading Perspectives on the New Global Paradigm

www.2012MultimediaEbook.com

Coupon Code – Book 4

The Wealth Garden

The New Dynamics of Wealth Creation in a Fast-Changing Global Economy

www.WealthGardenBook.com

Coupon Code – Book 3

You can purchase the print versions of
all these books at Amazon.com.